W9-BSX-038

upscale DOWNHOME

upscale DOWNHOME

family recipes, *all gussied up*

Rachel Hollis

Thomas Dunne Books
St. Martin's Griffin
New York

JESSAMINE COUNTY PUBLIC LIBRARY
600 South Main Street
Nicholasville, KY 40356
(859)885-3523

THOMAS DUNNE BOOKS.
An imprint of St. Martin's Press.

UPSCALE DOWNHOME. Copyright © 2016 by Rachel Hollis. All rights
reserved. Printed in China. For information, address St. Martin's
Press, 175 Fifth Avenue, New York, N.Y. 10010.

www.thomasdunnebooks.com
www.stmartins.com

Photographed by Jonathan Melendez and Cortnee Loren Brown
Designed by Cortnee Loren Brown

Production manager: Adriana Coada

The Library of Congress Cataloging-in-Publication Data is
available upon request.

ISBN 978-1-250-07884-1 (trade paperback)
ISBN 978-1-4668-9138-8 (e-book)

Our books may be purchased in bulk for promotional,
educational, or business use. Please contact your local
bookseller or the Macmillan Corporate and Premium Sales
Department at 1-800-221-7945, extension 5442, or by e-mail
at MacmillanSpecialMarkets@macmillan.com.

First Edition: October 2016

10 9 8 7 6 5 4 3 2 1

for mama,
who taught me that food is
the greatest love language

CONTENTS

upscale DOWNHOME

when I was twelve years old I hosted my first party. It was a luau in my friend Ashley's backyard and it was basically one big elaborate ruse to wear a grass skirt in front of a boy named Brian. I had been in love with Brian for years—or at least as deeply in love as you can be in sixth grade—and the party seemed like the perfect way to establish a deeper connection. Sadly for me, and my grass skirt, Brian spent most of that summer evening doing cannonballs instead of paying attention to me. Can you imagine my chagrin? There I was in my best Kmart two-piece, rocking my vanilla-flavored Lip Smackers; my side pony was totally on point, and he didn't look at me even once! I'll be honest, it was the first time I failed to lock in a new boyfriend over processed snack food, but sadly, not the last.

Bright side? I *did* discover a lifelong love for hosting parties. Oh sure, I was *familiar* with parties. I had grown up with parents who loved to entertain, but that luau was the first time I'd tried it on my own. It gave me a hint of what it was like to pick out invitations and design a theme. I chose Hawaiian Punch as our beverage (something my twelve-year-old brain thought was terribly witty), and kebabs as our appetizer. In the days before Pinterest, or, gosh, even the Internet (man, that makes me feel old!), it was a highly thematic party and I was utterly proud of myself. So what started as a ploy toward preteen romance became a lifelong passion.

That passion is why I still love to entertain at home. I love parties and potlucks. I love family dinners and cocktails with my friends on the back patio. I love Sunday suppers and Taco Tuesdays and celebrating on any day that ends in *Y*. I love the food, the wine, and having friends and family and people from all walks of life come together in one well-decorated space. I love giving people something to look forward to. I love sharing recipes. I love *ooh*ing and *aah*ing over Mema's carrot cake or discussing how adding the sweet basil really set off the flavors in Daddy's spaghetti sauce. I love themes, and cocktail napkins, and finding the perfect platter to display the turkey. I love all of these things, because everyone I know loves them, too. If there are people out there who don't enjoy a great meal with their loved ones—I've never met them!—maybe that's just because they haven't been to my house.

i grew up in a family full of loud Okie expats who migrated to Southern California during the dust bowl. It was by way of these characters—my grandpa Bill, my grandma Opal, Mema, and Papa and a menagerie of aunts, uncles, and cousins—that I learned to cook (and eat) at an early age. In our southern culture, *everything* revolved around food: What were we cooking? Who was bringing what to the potluck? Where would we celebrate Christmas dinner this year? Sharing a meal with the people I love has always been an integral part of my life. And because of this, food and I go together like peanut butter and jelly, like cheese and crackers, like a chocolate sundae with a side of fries . . . it just makes sense.

My family and I lived in a tiny pink parsonage on the outskirts of a small town on a street called Weedpatch Highway (yep, you read that right). As the baby of four, I had an unlimited supply of hand-me-down clothes, and even though my small hometown is in California, I spoke with the same thick twang as all of my southern relatives. So, as you might guess, the phrase "formal entertaining" wasn't part of our vernacular. Honestly, we didn't even have a word for it. My family just always had people over, always threw parties, and always made the biggest, fattest deal out of every holiday and birthday. And regardless of how much (or frankly, little) money we had, everyone was welcome. We weren't the Brady Bunch—far from it in fact. But those Christmases, those barbecues, those Sunday suppers are some of the most precious memories I have of my childhood. It was how I learned to show love: by cooking, by baking, by welcoming guests into our home, by setting the table with our mismatched china. Even on a random weeknight, there was always room for celebration.

at the ripe old age of seventeen, I moved to Los Angeles to become an actress and marry Matt Damon (in that order). I quickly lost interest in acting when I realized it required the complete expulsion of carbohydrates from my diet, and as for Matt . . . well, my real-life Prince Charming turned out to be much cuter. I met Dave Hollis when I was nineteen years old and he was twenty-seven. He was smart and funny and so, so tall, and we were very best friends from day one. When I looked at him I saw sunshine glowing around his head like magic and I could just make out the sound of a choir of baby angels singing his praises. When he looked at me he might have seen all kinds of things, but he couldn't get past the most obvious—my age. He was absolutely too old for me, he said. He was absolutely not interested in me, he assured. It took me about a year and a half to convince him he was wrong on both counts. We've been happily married for twelve years.

L.A. did prove lucrative in other ways, too. I launched my company, Chic Events, there in January of 2004. My company started out small: me, myself, and the occasional rogue intern working out of the basement of my town house, using my cell phone as an office line, and taking all client meetings at the local Starbucks. I used pictures from my own wedding to build a Web site and begged my friends and family for referrals. I devoured magazines of every kind: wedding, architecture, fashion, interior design—anything that might give me ideas on planning events in a fresh, new way. I worked hard to make my work original rather than regurgitating the same candelabra over and over again.

As a result my design aesthetic, just like my big southern family, is eclectic. I love bright, bold pops of color and mixing luxury pieces with something I found in the bargain bin. I love stylish design, but I'm a busy mother of three little boys so it also has to be comfortable and practical. You can see this sense of style weave its way through my early portfolio of work all the way to the posts on my Web site, the Chic Site, today.

This mix of my downhome roots and an upscale aesthetic has become my signature, but in the beginning it wasn't a style choice. Like all the coolest things, it was born out of necessity. When I booked those first client events years ago, I was doing parties for pennies and struggling to throw brides their dream wedding on a five-dollar budget. That meant I had to organize my spending around one or two *splurge* elements (like gorgeous floral or luxury linens), and then find a way to pull off the rest of the event for next to nothing. Those experiences were crucial to the creativity in designs and recipes I use today. When you don't have much to work with, you become an expert at squeezing water from a stone. Eventually, I'd squeezed enough water that Chic Events became a high-end luxury party-planning business, even though "high-end" and "luxury" couldn't be further from where I started out.

Let me share a story. The first time I heard the term "white trash" was when another girl called me that on the playground. I wasn't even sure what the term meant, but I understood her tone enough to have my feelings hurt. I knew that I didn't dress like the other girls or speak like the other girls, but for the first time I realized that this was a *bad thing*. It made me feel *other,* and somehow less than them. Isn't it amazing how something painful in our childhood can shape so much of who we become? The shame associated with those words would follow me through adolescence and into adulthood. When I moved to Los Angeles, I decided I would make a fresh start. I did everything I could to change myself into someone different. I learned how to dress and how to speak. I distinctly remember being at a party, letting a "y'all" slip into the conversation, and being utterly mortified that it had happened. It seems so silly in retrospect, but I didn't want to be *other* anymore; I wanted to fit in. I was terrified that my cool new friends in L.A. would judge me if they knew where I came from. Of course, what I've learned over time is that it's nearly impossible to find true success when you're pretending to be someone you're not. Another life lesson? Anyone who judges you for the town you grew up in or the bend of your accent is lame. You should run far and fast in the other direction.

Also, you will never find peace unless you feel truly comfortable being exactly who you are. It doesn't matter what clothes I wear or which mannerisms I adopt. I will always be a little girl from Weedpatch Highway. That doesn't make me better or worse than anyone else; it just makes me who I am.

Who I am is someone who loves dip recipes and cocktails served in Mason jars. It still tickles me pink that I've somehow managed to turn that passion for melted cheese into a career. But figuring out how to build a business around the food I love was really a happy accident. I had been running my events company for years when I decided to start a blog to market it to prospective clients. At the time, I thought it would be a great way to show off my luxury lifestyle designs because I was still trying to fit into an ideal of who I thought I should be. I had no idea what blogging was. I literally wrote about what I ate for dinner the night before. It wasn't a surprise when I had only one reader—my mom. I would share a post about cool centerpieces from a celebrity wedding or the cocktail hour setup from a movie premiere and no matter how much I tried to be fancy, nobody cared. Then one day, without anything better to write about, I posted a dip recipe that I'd loved in childhood, and it got an incredible response. I couldn't believe that people responded to something as simple as mayo-based dip, but they totally did. Luckily, I had a lifetime of recipes just like that one and I decided to share more.

I quickly discovered that, while the average person might enjoy lusting after million-dollar events in magazines, they certainly weren't throwing their own. Instead, readers *loved* it when I posted recipes made in a slow cooker, simple casseroles, inexpensive decor, items from the dollar bin, and anything topped with sour cream. Years removed from the unconfident girl I had been, I embraced the idea. I mixed the two ideals, luxury and down-home, and set out to prove that it's possible to do *anything* beautifully and with style. So,

I shifted the focus of my company solely to running the Chic Site. It's been an incredible, wild, and, to be honest, stressful journey, but it has provided me with so much joy . . . and unlimited access to baked goods.

I like to describe the Chic Site as my digital front porch. What I mean by that is, if we were girlfriends and we were hanging out on my front porch, these are the things we'd chat about over sweet tea: parenting our hoodlums, our marriages, everyone else's marriages, that casserole we made for dinner last night, our favorite cocktail, our favorite book, how torturous Spanx are, how we style our hair . . . basically, if it's interesting to women, that's what I cover. I hope the content inspires our readers. I hope the content is aspirational. But, more than anything, I want what I share on the Chic Site and in this book to be *achievable*. I want to show the pretty things—the perfectly styled room or the gorgeous layer cake or a hand-muddled cocktail. I also want to show you the truth. The truth is that I've struggled with postpartum depression. The truth is that sometimes I'm so busy chasing after my boys that I don't get a chance to shower. The truth is that I have stretch marks from three pregnancies, and while our living room is pretty, our garage looks like a bomb went off in there. The Chic Site and *Upscale Downhome* are not for women who live perfectly styled lives. Instead, they are for the authentic women, the honest women, the bright and joyful and messy and struggling everyday women. Because if we ever meet in real life, I hope you'd use those same words to describe me.

years ago I stumbled across the word "chic" in an old dictionary. Chic was defined as "a fashionable lifestyle, ideology, or pursuit." I fell in love with the word and the idea that chic is the pursuit of something better, prettier, or cooler than you are today. It's about wanting to be something greater than you are, to be more beautiful inside and out, and to live a more joyful life. Some days that might just mean something small, like putting the takeout on a real plate before you eat it. Other days that might mean something big, like agreeing to host Thanksgiving when you've never even *seen* a whole turkey, let alone cooked one. Chic isn't a state of being or even a destination; chic is the journey you take on the way to something greater. And for a little girl who once felt so awkward and different on the playground and worked so hard to make it here, that is incredibly poignant to me.

"Here" is in Los Angeles with my husband who happens to be the cutest and most hilarious man I've ever met. We have three equally handsome/hilarious little boys named Jackson, Sawyer, and Ford, and we spend most of our time doing super cool/sexy things like going to soccer practice and hitting up any restaurant where kids eat free with the purchase of an adult entrée. I work full time and then I come home and run around with my hair on fire trying to take care of my boys. I am the first to tell you that there are days I can't

even remember to brush my teeth, let alone cook something special or invite people over for dinner. But I know from experience that there will also be days when you *do* have time. There will be moments when you have a little extra wiggle room and you can push yourself to try something new. This book is for those moments. This book is for, *what should I make for dinner tonight?* This book is for, *how should we celebrate Mama's birthday this year?*

This book is for, *maybe we should do something special.* Because the truth is, this book is a gateway. The more you try out something new when you have an excuse, the more comfortable you'll feel trying out something new for any old reason at all.

last weekend, I was chatting with one of my girlfriends
and she told me she'd made dinner for her and her husband.

"Oh, what did you make?" I asked, because food is my love language.
"Oh, just a meat loaf and some mashed potatoes," she told me.
Just a *meat loaf?*
Just a meat loaf?
There's no such thing as just a meat loaf.

If you're going to take the time to prepare a recipe at home it isn't ever *just* a dish, it's an experience. Whether it's for twelve people or two, or just you and your cat, the fact that you put the effort into the preparation made it something special. You're *already* creating something beautiful. You're *already* hosting. You're *already* entertaining, even if you don't realize it. What I hope you'll do—what I hope this book encourages you to do—is go one extra step further. Add one unexpected ingredient or take the extra minute to put your dish on a pretty tray. Trying just a little bit harder is the definition of chic, remember? So flex your hosting muscles and up your game!

So many lifestyle brands focus on what you need to do, have, or buy in order to be stylish. I believe that, just like Dorothy and her ruby slippers, you've always had the power. You just have to learn how to use it. Instead of hiring a florist and trying to create haute cuisine from scratch, why not embrace the recipes you grew up loving, the china you never actually use, and those roses in your backyard? I know what you're thinking—you're thinking,

I don't know any recipes, my "china" is from the dollar store, and I have no earthly clue how to make a flower arrangement. Guess what, guys, I can help you with all of those things! I do know recipes, and how to make a flower arrangement, and I too own ninety-nine-cent dinner plates but I know how to make those suckers *look good*. Think of me as your favorite well-organized aunt or your really crafty cousin or your friend Kelly who bakes the best cupcakes—except, unlike your aunt, I don't use Aqua Net or read Harlequin novels. Actually, that's a lie, I totally read Harlequin novels. I can't help it, I'm a sucker for any love story involving a secret baby—but that's not the point. The point is this experience should be fun. Throw on an apron (preferably vintage), throw back a cocktail (for courage), and give it a try. No one ever complains if their party host has a snafu, and if they do, you don't want that meanie for a friend anyway.

so you're going to entertain, or make lasagna for you and your husband or cat or whoever, and now you're wondering, when should I use these recipes? Maybe the better question is, when should you *not* use these recipes? The idea behind this cookbook is that it's filled with real, everyday dishes, but they're presented beautifully. So you can use them for a weeknight dinner or that bridal shower you're hosting for your best friend. The recipe, the name, or the ingredients (and sometimes all three) for each dish is so polished you'd never know it was likely dreamed up in a trailer park. Everything you'll find in here is beautifully presented, but every recipe is also practical. Practical is key because so many cookbooks are the food equivalent of a white sofa. Let me explain. Whenever I see a white sofa in a design magazine, I swoon. It's so pretty, and it looks so posh in the gorgeous room it's sitting in. But, if I ever attempted that in my own home you and I both know that my kids would get blood or chocolate or Play-Doh (or possibly all three) on that white sofa in less time than it takes to hard-boil an egg. A white sofa isn't practical for my life, just like a lot of other cookbooks aren't practical for my life. I think it's magical to make your own chicken stock. It's incredible to grow your own root vegetables and keep a starter in your fridge so you can have fresh homemade bread every day.

But, gentle reader, that's just not my jam.

So I share recipes that are. Rather than the typical cookbook recipe sections, I've used categories such as "Slow Cooker," "Potluck," "Somethin' Sweet," and "Leftovers." This is pee-my-pants food—as in, it's so good it makes me want to pee my pants. These are the dishes I make for the people I love because I hope it makes them want to pee their pants, too. I serve the Green Chicken Enchiladas whenever new friends come for dinner, because I haven't yet met someone who doesn't like a fiesta. The Jalapeño Popper Dip and the Spicy Corn Dip battle for favorite snack at any Hollis family party. The Jell-O Pretzel Salad, which despite its name is actually not a salad in any way, shape, or form, is the most popular dessert

I know, hands down. The Wassail has been the centerpiece of our holiday party for as long as I can remember. From beginning to end, each of these dishes makes up a special memory in my heart. I hope they'll find their way into your heart—and your kitchen—as well.

In addition to recipes, I've also included a party section at the back of the book.

This is a collection of my favorite ways to celebrate in my real life. I'll show you some visual inspirations and a dream menu for each type of party using the recipes from earlier chapters. You can use it if you already have a party on the books and just need some ideas. You can use it if you're looking for a reason to celebrate and want to come up with a theme. You can use it to re-create these parties exactly or just as a place to learn a few new tricks. But remember, there's no such thing as *just* a meat loaf, and if you're going to go to the work of creating something tasty, why not use that as a chance to celebrate life?

Because that's what entertaining is, it's celebrating life. You entertain because it is such an incredible way to build a sense of community for yourself and your family. You entertain because throwing a shower or a birthday party is a great way to spoil your best friend who so richly deserves it. You entertain because a Super Bowl party with all his favorite foods can mean a lot to your husband. There are so many wonderful reasons to entertain in your home, but the greatest I know is this: Life is short.

The weekend before my big brother died, we had a party. It was a Sunday in late September, and Daddy came home and announced that he'd invited everyone over, *just because*. It's funny the things you remember from moments like that. I remember a big trip to the grocery store for things to cook. I remember swimming all afternoon with my cousins. I remember the menu we whipped up for our family and friends and that it was the first and only time I ever saw my aunt Linda try champagne. It was pink, and I couldn't wait to be old enough to try some, too. We laughed and talked and people came and went all afternoon. A few days later, Ryan was gone.

I believe in my heart that someday he and I will be together again, that we'll talk and laugh and, if heaven allows, share our own glass of pink champagne. But that doesn't make this time without him any easier. It doesn't mean it wasn't devastating that he didn't dance with me on my wedding day. It doesn't make it less painful that he's never attended any of my sons' birthday parties. I think of this a lot when people ask me why I celebrate every chance I get. The answer is as simple as this—tomorrow isn't a guarantee.

Break out the good china because it's Tuesday. Make your husband's favorite casserole because he beat you at Scrabble. Celebrate Mondays and Wednesdays and half birthdays. Celebrate babies and grandparents and when your eighth-grader passes chemistry. Celebrate

Easter, Thanksgiving, Kwanzaa, and Rosh Hashanah. Celebrate for any and every reason, because you don't know the next time you'll have an opportunity to celebrate and that in itself is reason enough. Today is a precious gift, and that gift is something to be celebrated.

where should you entertain? why, any old place at all!

All of my favorite childhood memories are centered on a party or gathering we had as a family. Nearly every single one of those parties was in the little red two-bedroom house that my grandparents lived in. For each of our holidays and birthdays we'd cram fifty people into a home that could comfortably fit only a handful. It was loud, there was never anywhere to sit, and between the body count and my grandparents' need to always blast the furnace, the temperature inside rivaled Death Valley for the hottest place in the continental United States. And you know what? Nobody cared. Everyone was happy to be there to gossip and grumble and share a meal. We were excited to eat Uncle Joe's half-moon pies or Grandma Neeley's cherry chip cake, and the location was entirely irrelevant.

I wish we could all escape the mentality that you need the perfect house in order to have people over. Inviting friends and family into your home is one of the best gifts you can give someone else. It is the greatest measure of respect to prepare a meal for another person. Recently my friend Katie was describing someone from church I hadn't met, and she said, "Oh, they're actually really good friends of ours. Like, hang-out-in-the-kitchen-while-dinner-finishes-cooking kind of friends." And I thought to myself, yes, that's it exactly! The dinner table is sacred, and inviting someone to gather around it allows them inside your life in a way they'll never have access to otherwise, no matter how much you keep up with their life on Facebook. It's a real, honest attempt to share your life and build a community with those around you. So whether you're in a mansion or an apartment or a trailer park, it's not about where you're hosting. It's about the warm home you welcome your guests into.

not sure how to even begin having someone over? Well, let's talk about where you start. You start with the Boy Scout motto: *Always Be Prepared.*

You need to begin collecting a menagerie of hosting paraphernalia. Just like a warrior wouldn't go into battle without the proper armor, you, too, must be armed and ready to handle whatever the recipe or event might throw at you. If you gave me half an hour's notice that you were dropping by my house for an impromptu cocktail, a home-cooked meal, or to introduce me to a visiting maharaja, I would be ready to wow you by the time you arrived. This isn't because I've got a chef and a florist at my disposal. It's because I've collected an arsenal of platters, plates, wineglasses, unique liqueurs, vintage pinots, specialty mixed nuts, and the knowledge of at least four different ways to turn regular old cheese into something divine. I've used them all countless times in countless ways to entertain people just like you. I've got a bag of tricks, and I'm constantly adding to it. So when the situation presents itself, of course you can drop by, nothing would make me happier.

the list

Whether you're just starting out or adding to your current collection, here are the items every host and hostess should always have on hand. I don't tell you this so you'll run out and buy everything tomorrow. These are just items to keep an eye out for when you see them on sale. My favorite places to find them? The sales rack at my favorite stores such as Target, Anthropologie, Walmart, or HomeGoods. But "new" doesn't mean better. Don't count out previously loved treasures from the flea market, the Goodwill, yard sales, or your grandma's china hutch. If you can't afford them now, keep a running list of your dream item and ask for one or two for Christmas or your birthday. I had a Le Creuset Dutch oven on my Christmas list for three years before Santa finally clued in and got me one. Also, please don't think you need a million of everything. If you look closely in this book, you'll see that I use the same pieces over and over again.

1. Solid Color Dinnerware Set. At a minimum, aim for a place setting for every member of your immediate family. If you can afford it, try for eight to ten place settings if not more. And don't worry if it's not real china. Remember, I have a set of deep green dinner plates I bought at the 99¢ Only Store when I was nineteen and I still use them every Christmas.

2. Silverware Set. Ideally you want at least one set to go with every dinnerware set you have, but it's the more the merrier as far as silverware is concerned. Also don't forget serving utensils: large spoons, forks, tongs, etc. I'm forever running out of these at potlucks so I finally just bought a ton of serving spoons at the dollar store and keep them stored in the garage for when I need them.

3. Pedestal Cake Plate. You can use this to display your dessert, hold your centerpiece, or add height to your buffet.

4. Platters. These can be any color or texture, but if you try to find similar hues or materials, you'll be able to mix and match them easily with a variety of other designs.

5. Appetizer Plates. Have fun with these since they are usually used in a fun setting. My favorite collection is a brown zebra print. I also have a handful of plates in different shades of white that I pair with the gorgeous hand-painted china that Mema gave me.

6. Small Serving Dishes. These may seem like a splurge for something you won't use that often, but rest assured that I'm always finding little parfait glasses, oversized ceramic spoons, ramekins, and more on clearance. Serving a classic dish in small individual portions is an easy way to reinvent your favorites.

7. Linen Cocktail Napkins. Mine are all mixed and matched because I usually find two or three fun options in the clearance rack. As long as they're a similar hue, they can be used together.

8. Linen Dinner Napkins. You should have more than the number of your dinnerware set in case someone drops one on the floor. Also, unless you're much more graceful than I am, I'd stay away from white and ivory since sadly some stains never come out.

9. Red Wine Glasses. When it comes to red wine, the bigger the balloon the better.

10. White Wine Glasses. Find something to complement the red wine glasses. The easiest way is to purchase them together, but if that's not an option just look for something with a similar style, height, and color.

11. Martini Shaker. A necessity if you're a cocktail aficionado, or at least aspire to be. Extra credit if you go full bartender flair like Tom Cruise in *Cocktail*.

12. Low Ball Glasses. I use these for everything: liquor, margaritas, martinis—they're so versatile. In a pinch they can also be a votive holder or a vase for small arrangements.

13. Straws. I know it seems like a small thing, but whenever I serve a drink with a fun matching straw my guests get so excited. When you don't have a big budget you can't always have the fanciest glass or the nicest liquor, but a sweet little accessory can elevate your drink for only a few pennies.

14. Well-Stocked Bar. Start with vodka, rum, gin, whiskey, tonic, soda water, triple sec, lime juice, and lemon juice. Always have a great bottle of red and a great bottle of white—you can save the fancy bottle your boss gave you for Christmas or keep an eye out for a sale at your local wine store.

15. Proper Wine Opener. A sommelier wine opener is the best one you can use and poses the lowest risk of breaking your cork. If you want to use something else, just make sure it's a true corkscrew (looks like a pig's tail) instead of the cheap versions that look more like a drill bit.

16. Glass Pitcher. Iced tea, lemonade, spa water, sangria, flowers, a goldfish . . . You can put anything in there! Once during a housewarming I used my glass pitcher to hold the silverware and everyone thought it was adorable . . . actually, I'd just run out of containers.

17. Assorted Glass Vases. I have varying sizes and shapes that I use for everything from centerpieces to food displays to silverware holders. Collect these from garage sales and flea markets.

18. Well-Stocked Pantry. Stock up on nonperishable ingredients you can serve in a pinch: mixed nuts, olives, tortilla chips, cookies, chocolates, and crackers make great snacks. Keeping things like balsamic vinegar, olive oil, specialty salsa, and honey on hand can help to enhance flavor and take a simple last-minute appetizer to the next level. I like to store my extra pantry items in a basket high up on a shelf, so nobody "accidentally" eats something I've been saving for guests.

19. Tablecloths. You need at least one great cloth that covers your table properly and fits in nicely with the room and the dinnerware. I buy mine on clearance after the holidays and store them on hangers in my front closet so they're relatively wrinkle free when I need them.

20. Kitchen Twine. I use mine for everything from trussing chicken to hanging up lanterns. It's great in place of ribbon for some rustic wrapping paper, and on occasion, it's been used as a zip line for my three-year-old's action figures.

21. Votive Candles. These are the easiest way to add ambiance to any room and they come in every size, shape, and color you can imagine.

22. Duct Tape. Every event planner's best friend. It can fix anything from a broken pipe to a hem line, and once, in an extreme emergency, it held a bride's dress together as she walked down the aisle (but that's another book).

23. Birthday Candles. You'll be happy to have them on hand the one time you forget. I did forget once . . . for my second son's first birthday. My husband had to run to the store during the party and I felt like the world's worst mom, so just take my advice on this one, people.

24. Music. Whether it's an iPod, a collection of CDs, or your own a cappella rendition of "Dixieland Delight," you need music at your party. I keep several different playlists on hand: There's the Cuban band I play when I want some Latin flair and the old standards we'll listen to over martinis. There's even a playlist on my phone called Country in the Summer Air. The title is a bit lofty, but it's perfect for beers on the back patio. Just remember, the music can set the tone for the entire event.

25. Chilled Bottle of Champagne. There are so many great moments to celebrate in life, and if you set yourself up to celebrate in style, it's going to motivate you to look for opportunities to pop that cork. Also, consider using that same champagne as a motivator *to* entertain. I like to put little tags on my champagne with notes like "Adoption Paperwork Gets Turned In" or "*Upscale Downhome* Comes Out." Every time I see the tag I remember that something exciting is on the horizon.

clearance button-down from the target boys' section

inexpensive white bowls from 99-cent store

keep fun toothpicks on hand to jazz up your apps

snacks

It was a little difficult figuring out how best to describe this section. At first glance, you may see these as appetizers for your next party, but then you find something like Broccoli Cheddar Garlic Pull-Apart Bread and you think, *Well, shoot, what if I don't want to wait for a party to have that bread? What if I just want something to nosh while I watch Netflix tonight with my hubby?* So, I went with Snacks because you should call on these recipes anytime you want to nibble on something tasty. It's a collection of bite-size food so good it'll make your toes curl and your arm hair stand at attention . . . or maybe I'm the only one carbs affect that way. Some of the recipes are a reinvention of an old classic. Some are totally made up by my family over the years. All of them are great.

SNACKS

PIGS in a *blanket*

this is an appetizer that never disappoints, especially when you upgrade your hot dogs for some great sausage instead. Honestly, I can't think of a party where I've ever had any left over, regardless of how many I started with.

Makes about 30

INGREDIENTS

2 frozen puff pastry sheets, thawed
2 (12-ounce) packages of smoked beef or pork sausage, cut into 1-inch pieces
1 large egg, whisked with a splash of water
1 teaspoon freshly cracked black pepper
¼ cup whole-grain mustard
2 tablespoons honey

PREPARATION

1. Preheat the oven to 375°F. Line a baking sheet with parchment paper and set aside.

2. Cut each puff pastry sheet into thirds and then into small strips—long enough to roll around a piece of sausage. Roll the pastry around the sausage and seal the edges. Place seam side down on the prepared baking sheet.

3. Brush each pastry liberally with egg wash and sprinkle with freshly cracked black pepper. Bake for 20 to 25 minutes or until golden brown. Remove from the oven and serve with honey-mustard dipping sauce. These can be made in advance and stored in the freezer. Just reheat in the oven before eating.

4. To make the dipping sauce, in a small bowl, whisk the mustard and honey until smooth. The sauce can be made ahead and stored in the fridge.

put dipping sauce into a small container and rest the pig on top for a cute display. xo

*linguica-*STUFFED
mushrooms

1ST PLACE

LINGUISA STUFFED
MUSHROOMS

Sheree Neeley
Bakersfield

24 fresh mushrooms
½ cup diced linguisa
1 small onion, finely chopped
2 tbsp. mayonnaise
½ cup shredded mozzarella
    cheese

Wash and pat dry mushrooms.
Remove stems. Finely chop
stems. In medium skillet, saute
stems, onions and linguisa for 3
minutes. Drain thoroughly. In a
small bowl mix stems, onion,
linguisa with mayonnaise and
cheese. Stuff caps with mixture.
Bake at 325° for 15-20 minutes.

Sheree Neeley

this is such a special recipe for me because it's one of the dishes that made my mom famous. By "famous," I mean that she won a prize for it and was featured in our hometown newspaper back in the '80s. As a five-year-old I remember seeing her picture in print and thinking she was the coolest person I knew. Twenty-eight years later, my opinion hasn't changed.

Makes 24 mushrooms

INGREDIENTS

24 fresh white button mushrooms
1 small onion, finely chopped
½ cup diced linguica sausage
3 tablespoons mayonnaise
¾ cup shredded mozzarella cheese

PREPARATION

1. Preheat the oven to 350°F. Wash and pat dry the mushrooms. Remove and finely chop the stems.

2. In a medium skillet, sauté stems, onion, and linguica over medium-high heat for 3 minutes. Drain thoroughly.

3. In a small bowl, mix the cooked stems, onion, and linguica with mayonnaise and cheese.

4. Stuff the mushroom caps with the mixture and arrange on a baking sheet.

5. Bake for 15 to 20 minutes. Allow to cool slightly before eating.

this pull-apart bread is the perfect appetizer for a newbie hostess since you don't need much kitchen prowess to pull it off. If you own a knife and have the ability to melt cheese, you're about twenty minutes away from flavor town!

Makes 6 to 8 servings

INGREDIENTS

1½ cups broccoli pieces
1 round sourdough bread loaf
¼ pound (1 stick) unsalted butter, melted
3 garlic cloves, minced
½ teaspoon Italian seasoning
¼ teaspoon crushed red pepper flakes
1½ cups shredded Cheddar cheese
1 scallion, chopped (about 2 tablespoons)

PREPARATION

1. Preheat the oven to 350°F. Line a baking sheet with foil and set aside. Steam the broccoli. You can do this in a steamer or place the broccoli in a bowl with a ¼ cup of water and cover with plastic wrap. Cut a few holes in the plastic wrap to vent. Cook in the microwave for 5 minutes.

2. Slice a crisscross pattern into the top of the bread, creating ½-inch cubes, but don't slice all the way through. Stop about a ½ inch from the bottom of the bread. Transfer the bread to the foil-lined baking sheet.

3. In a small bowl, combine melted butter, garlic, Italian seasoning, and crushed red pepper flakes. Pour the mixture over the bread, separating the bread with your fingers to allow the sauce to fall between the cubes. Make sure the entire bread is coated with the butter sauce. Distribute the minced garlic evenly, tucking it between the cubes. Stuff the broccoli pieces between the cubes of the bread. Bake for 10 minutes.

4. Remove the bread from the oven and allow to cool slightly. Sprinkle with the Cheddar cheese, making sure to tuck some of the cheese in between the cubes as well. Sprinkle with the scallion and return to the oven to bake for another 12 minutes, until the cheese has melted and the bread has browned. Remove from the oven and serve warm.

broccoli
cheddar
GARLIC
pull-apart
BREAD

turkey AND ham pinwheels

pinwheels were always a staple at our family parties because they're tasty and age-appropriate. Meaning, no matter what age you are you're going to think they're appropriate. The bummer is I've always struggled with how to make them pretty enough to sit alongside all of the other pretty food on the buffet. By using some unique tortillas and flavorful ingredients, I turned this homely classic into a standout dish.

Makes 4 to 6 servings

INGREDIENTS

4 spinach flour tortillas
4 sun-dried tomato flour tortillas
½ cup ranch dressing
12 slices provolone cheese
12 slices mozzarella cheese
12 slices turkey lunch meat
12 slices ham lunch meat
1 (16-ounce) jar roasted red peppers, drained
1 cup sliced black olives, drained
2 cups baby spinach
1 cup dill pickle slices

PREPARATION

1. In a dry skillet, warm the tortillas over medium heat to make them pliable.

2 & 3. Spread each tortilla with ranch dressing and then layer with the different filling options.

4. Roll into a tight log and continue filling and rolling the rest of the tortillas.

5. Slice into pinwheels and serve.

these also make a great lunch or after-school snack for the kiddos! xo

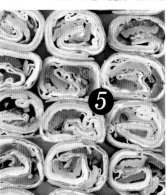

french *onion* SOUP bites

let's be honest, the best part of French onion soup is the cheesy crouton on top, right? Who really cares about the soup once you've eaten through the gratin? This appetizer gives you what you want—a tasty bite of bread soaked with French onion soup and then baked with cheese to devour all in one bite. It's, in a word, incredible.

Makes 4 to 6 servings

INGREDIENTS

1 packet French onion soup mix
2 tablespoons olive oil
1 medium yellow onion, chopped
1 pound white button mushrooms, sliced
½ teaspoon salt
¼ teaspoon black pepper
2 tablespoons flour
1 loaf Asiago cheese French bread
½ cup shredded Gruyère cheese

PREPARATION

1. Preheat the oven to 350°F. In a stockpot, cook the French onion soup per package instructions.

2. In a large skillet, heat the olive oil. Add the onion and mushrooms and cook over medium-high heat for 5 to 8 minutes or until the onion just begins to caramelize. Season with salt and pepper. Remove the veggies from the skillet and set aside.

3. In the skillet, create a roux by adding the flour to your existing olive oil (this just means whisking the flour around in the oil until it creates a thick lumpy paste) over medium-high heat. Add the soup broth to the roux while whisking. Next add in the mushrooms and onions and cook for about 15 minutes, until thickened and cooked down somewhat.

4. Meanwhile, cut the loaf of bread into large cubes and arrange in a baking dish. Bake for about 10 minutes to begin to toast. Remove from the oven and cover with the thickened soup mixture. Flip each bread cube so that both sides are evenly coated. Cover the top generously with shredded cheese and bake for another 5 minutes, or until the cheese has melted and is bubbly. Arrange the bites on a plate or platter and skewer with a toothpick for guests.

when she found out about the snack section of this cookbook my big sister, Christina, said, "You know what you should include? Hot Dog Taquitos!" I told her that even though it was one of our favorites —another crazy recipe dreamed up by my mama—it might actually be *too* downhome. But then I thought about it and I figured some of you might love this as much as I do. If you've got a refined palate, just skip to the next page. But if you like a little county fair–style snack that's fried with cheese, take this out for a spin.

Makes 8 hot dogs

INGREDIENTS

8 medium flour tortillas
1 package (8) hot dogs
4 slices American cheese, cut in half
Vegetable oil

PREPARATION

1. In a dry skillet, warm the tortillas over medium heat, just to make them pliable.

2. Place one hot dog on each tortilla, along with half of a slice of American cheese. Fold the sides in and then roll into a tight *taquito*.

3. In a large skillet, heat about an inch of vegetable oil over medium heat. Once the oil is hot, fry the hot dogs seam side down a few at a time, until golden brown and flaky. Cook in batches. Place the hot dogs on a plate lined with paper towels to soak up the excess grease. Serve warm.

this is great with corn or flour tortillas. xo

hot DOG taquitos

FRIED *okra*
with
buttermilk ranch

where i come from, fried okra is a *big* deal. My mom made it, my grandparents made it, and everyone loved it except for me. It wasn't until I was older and decided to make it with Italian bread crumbs that I really understood the appeal. Italian bread crumbs add great flavor and awesome crunch. The buttermilk ranch? Well, that just makes *everything* better, right?

Makes 4 to 6 servings

INGREDIENTS

6 cups vegetable or canola oil, for frying
1 cup all-purpose flour
1 teaspoon seasoned salt
1 teaspoon garlic salt
2 cups buttermilk, divided
1 cup Italian-style bread crumbs
3 pounds fresh okra, sliced into ½-inch pieces
1 package buttermilk ranch dressing mix
1 cup sour cream

PREPARATION

1. Pour the oil in a large Dutch oven or pot and heat to about 350°F, over medium-high heat.

2. Pour the flour into a shallow dish and mix in the seasoned salt and garlic salt. Pour 1 cup buttermilk in another shallow dish and pour the bread crumbs into a third shallow dish. Coat the okra by first passing through the flour, then the buttermilk, and then the bread crumbs.

3. Fry the okra in batches in the hot oil until golden brown and crispy. Transfer the okra to a plate lined with paper towels to soak up any excess oil.

4. In a small bowl, stir the ranch dressing mix along with the remaining 1 cup buttermilk and sour cream until smooth. Serve with the okra for dipping.

sticky HAM'n'CHEESE

everybody's grandma, cousin, aunt, and mama is positive she invented this recipe. Depending on where you're from, you might know them as Sister Becky's Sandwiches or Auntie Heather's Ham 'n' Swiss. The name changes from place to place, but this classic is *always* delicious.

Makes 15 sandwiches

INGREDIENTS

15 King's Hawaiian sweet dinner rolls
½ cup mayonnaise
30 slices deli ham
15 slices Swiss cheese, cut in half
1 tablespoon poppy seeds
1½ tablespoons Dijon mustard
¼ pound (1 stick) unsalted butter, melted
1 tablespoon onion powder
1 teaspoon Worcestershire sauce

PREPARATION

1. Preheat the oven to 350°F.

2. Cut the rolls in half and spread mayonnaise onto one side of the roll. Place two slices of ham and two half slices of Swiss cheese in the roll.

3. Replace the top of the rolls and bunch the finished sandwiches closely together in a baking dish.

4. In a medium bowl, whisk together poppy seeds, Dijon mustard, melted butter, onion powder, and Worcestershire sauce.

5. Pour the sauce over the rolls, just covering the tops. Cover the dish with foil and let sit for 10 minutes.

6. Bake for 10 minutes or until cheese is melted. Uncover and cook for an additional 2 minutes until tops are slightly browned and crisp. Serve warm.

SPAM *and* pineapple skewers

don't hate on the spam!

Spam is delicious, and when I was growing up it was a huge treat to get a fried Spam sandwich on white bread with mayo. For a party, I like to turn it into kebabs. The key to making this dish look fancy? Cutting the meat in perfect squares and searing in those great grill marks so it looks pretty on the skewer.

Makes 4 to 6 servings

INGREDIENTS

Wooden skewers
2 cans Spam, cut into 2-inch cubes
2 cups fresh pineapple, cut into 2-inch cubes
2 tablespoons vegetable oil
¾ cup soy sauce
¼ cup pineapple juice
½ cup light brown sugar
¼ cup granulated sugar
2 tablespoons fresh ginger, peeled and grated
2 scallions, sliced

PREPARATION

1. Skewer the Spam and pineapple cubes, alternating between the two. Brush with oil and set aside.

2. In a small saucepan, combine the soy sauce, pineapple juice, light brown sugar, granulated sugar, ginger, and scallions. Cook over medium heat, stirring often, for about 15 minutes or until it has reduced by half.

3. Heat a stovetop or outdoor grill over medium-high heat. Place the skewers on the grill and cook for 4 to 5 minutes per side. Brush the skewers with the sauce and grill for another minute or two. Serve warm.

add more color to your skewer with bell peppers and onions. xo

these little bites are as darling as they are delicious. You just take all the classic ingredients for a BLT and shrink them down into this dainty little package. It's got bacon, thickly sliced bread, fresh lettuce, cherry tomato, and yummy pesto mayonnaise so good I could eat it by itself.

Makes 20 to 24 bites

INGREDIENTS

1 loaf white bread, unsliced
2 tablespoons olive oil
½ cup mayonnaise
2 tablespoons prepared pesto
8 to 10 iceberg lettuce leaves, chopped into chunks
1 pint cherry tomatoes
1 pound bacon, cooked until crispy
Long appetizer toothpicks

PREPARATION

1. Preheat the oven to 350°F.

2. Cut the bread into thick slices, about ½ inch thick, and then cut each slice into small squares. Place the squares onto a baking sheet and drizzle the olive oil on top and toss to fully coat. Spread in an even layer and bake for about 5 minutes or until golden brown and slightly crispy. Remove from the oven and allow to cool slightly.

3. In a small bowl, combine the mayonnaise and prepared pesto.

4. Spread some of the pesto mixture on top of each bread slice. Layer with lettuce, a cherry tomato, and crispy bacon on each. Skewer with a long toothpick to hold in place, but also to make it easier for your guests to grab. Serve at room temperature.

stock up on cute toothpicks whenever you see them on clearance. then you'll always have some on hand for appetizers. xo

BLT
bites

grilled guac! yum!

my kid's baseball tee!

my favorite app
plates & 99 cent
store napkins

my trusty jeans

dips

Dips are one of the most popular dishes that we feature on the Chic Site. In fact, it was a dip that made me realize how much my readers loved a downhome recipe. You know that spinach dip that you make using a packet from the salad dressing aisle? It's the one with peas and carrots in it and you mix it with spinach and a gallon of mayo and serve it in a bread bowl and it's delicious? Yeah, well, I love that dip. Years ago when I ran out of ideas for what I could blog about for my events company, I decided to blog about that dip and readers freaked out because they loved it, too. It was that post that planted a seed for the kind of content I wanted to create on my site. Because of that, we take our dips very seriously around these parts. This section is a collection of my favorite dips (deciding on them was like asking me to decide which of my children I love the most), and every single one of them is delicious. If you're lactose intolerant you might want to skip ahead because my love affair with cheese is on display throughout this chapter.

DIPS

jalapeño popper DIP

this also makes one heck of a sandwich spread... like on those blt bites on page 42 for instance! xo

i could eat a bowl of this as a meal. No, really! Don't dare me. The cheese makes it creamy and the panko crumbs add a great crunch. The jalapeño gives it a kick of spice and, since you grill them first, there's a great smoky flavor that permeates the whole thing. This dish is one of my go-to appetizers for any occasion.

Makes 8 to 12 servings

INGREDIENTS

12 fresh jalapeños, cut in half lengthwise and seeded
2 (8-ounce) packages cream cheese, softened
¾ cup mayonnaise
½ cup shredded Cheddar cheese
½ cup shredded Monterey Jack cheese
Couple of dashes of hot sauce (optional)
½ teaspoon salt
½ teaspoon black pepper
¾ cup panko bread crumbs

PREPARATION

1. Preheat oven to 375°F.

2. Heat a stovetop or outdoor grill over medium-high heat. Lightly grease the grill with cooking spray. Grill the cut jalapeños until charred, about 2 minutes per side. Remove from the heat and allow to cool. Give them a rough chop.

3. In a large bowl, mix the cream cheese, mayonnaise, Cheddar, Monterey Jack, hot sauce if using, chopped grilled jalapeños, salt, and black pepper until evenly combined.

4. Pour the dip into an 8- or 9-inch baking dish. Square or round will work. You can also use medium ramekins. Top the dip with the panko bread crumbs and bake for 20 to 25 minutes, until bubbly and golden brown on top.

5. Serve with veggies, crackers, or chips. Enjoy!

loaded
baked
potato
DIP

i adore a baked potato in any form. In fact, if I ever commit some heinous crime and it's the night before the firing squad, my last meal will be a loaded baked potato. In this recipe, I took a dish I liked and turned into an appetizer you're going to love. You're welcome!

//

Makes 8 to 12 servings

INGREDIENTS

8 slices bacon, sliced
2 small baking potatoes
1 (16-ounce) container sour cream
1 (8-ounce) container chive and garlic cream cheese, softened
½ cup whole milk
1/3 cup fresh chives, chopped, plus more for garnish
2 cups shredded Cheddar cheese, divided
½ teaspoon garlic powder

PREPARATION

1. Preheat the oven to 350°F. In a skillet, cook the bacon over medium heat until the fat has rendered and the bacon has crisped. Using a slotted spoon, transfer the bacon to a plate lined with paper towels to soak up excess fat. Set aside.

2. Cook the potatoes in a microwave until fork tender, about 8 to 10 minutes. Allow the potatoes to cool, then dice or shred using a box grater.

3. In a large bowl, combine the sour cream, cream cheese, milk, potatoes, chives, 1 cup of cheese, garlic powder, and the crisped bacon, reserving some bacon for garnish. Stir until evenly combined.

4. Transfer to a baking dish and top with the remaining cheese. Bake for 20 to 25 minutes or until warmed through and the cheese on top has melted.

5. Garnish with bacon and chives and serve immediately.

do you know what this

appetizer is, you guys? It's basically just really fancy-looking melted cheese! Add a little puff pastry and some fruit and not only is it delicious, but it looks like you put in much more effort than you actually did.

//

Makes 4 to 6 servings

INGREDIENTS

1 pint fresh blueberries
1 round of brie cheese
1 frozen puff pastry sheet, thawed
1 large egg, whisked with a splash of water
Sliced baguette or crackers for serving

PREPARATION

1. Preheat the oven to 350°F. Line a baking sheet with parchment paper and set aside.

2. Place a handful of blueberries on top of the brie round, reserving the remaining for serving. Then carefully wrap the puff pastry around the brie and berries, turning it over to seal the edges together.

3. Transfer to the prepared baking sheet and brush liberally with egg wash. Bake for 20 to 25 minutes or until the puff pastry is golden brown.

4. Remove from the oven and allow to cool slightly before serving.

5. Serve with toast or crackers, and remaining blueberries.

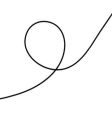

you can use any fresh fruit or perserves you have on hand. xo

BAKED
blueberry **brie**

BEAN *and* cheese DIP

at first glance there's not much to this recipe. In fact, it's just four store-bought ingredients mixed together in the right quantities and then baked. But even though it's simple, it's so good you'll kind of want to make out with it a little. Keep these ingredients on hand throughout the summer and you'll always have a ready-to-go appetizer.

//

Makes 8 to 12 servings

INGREDIENTS

4 (15-ounce) cans refried beans
1 (16-ounce) jar salsa
1 (4.5-ounce) can diced green chiles, drained
2 cups shredded Cheddar cheese

PREPARATION

1. Preheat the oven to 350°F.

2. In a large bowl, mix the beans, salsa, and diced green chiles.

3. Pour the mixture into an oven-safe casserole dish and sprinkle the top with the cheese.

4. Bake until warmed throughout and the cheese on top is melted, about 20 minutes.

mix this up with black beans or a cool salsa flavor! xo

we celebrate Fourth of July the same way every year, at my in-laws' house hunched over a big bowl of Chili Cheese Dip. Yes, there are other foods there as well, but this dip is always the star of the show. We make a big giant helping of it and every time it starts to cool off we pop it back in the oven to warm it up again. If you ask me, nothing says "American holiday" like eating piping hot chili cheese all day long.

Makes 8 to 12 servings

INGREDIENTS

2 (8-ounce) packages cream cheese, softened
1 (15-ounce) can chili (without beans)
1 cup shredded Cheddar cheese
1 small tomato, diced
1 scallion, sliced (about 2 tablespoons)

PREPARATION

1. Preheat oven to 350°F.

2. Spread the softened cream cheese in a single layer in a 8- or 9-inch square baking dish.

3. Top with the chili and spread in an even layer. Sprinkle cheese on top and bake for 20 to 25 minutes until bubbly and the cheese has melted.

4. Remove from oven and garnish with diced tomato and scallion. Serve immediately.

I serve this with tortilla chips or corn chips. xo

chili *cheese* DIP

pepperoni
PIZZA dip

use your favorite pizza toppings to make your version! xo

i'm pretty sure this one

needs no introduction because the photo alone is drool-worthy. This is a great app to serve at a game-day viewing party because there's something about watching sports that doesn't make us feel as guilty about the calories, right?

//

Makes 8 to 12 servings

INGREDIENTS

1 (8-ounce) package cream cheese, softened
1 (32-ounce) container ricotta cheese
1 large egg
1 teaspoon salt
1 teaspoon black pepper
½ teaspoon crushed red pepper flakes
½ teaspoon dried oregano
1 tablespoon olive oil
1 shallot, minced
2 garlic cloves, minced
1 red bell pepper, diced
1 pound crimini mushrooms, sliced
1½ cups pizza sauce
¼ cup grated Parmesan cheese
1½ cups shredded mozzarella cheese
8 to 12 slices pepperoni
1 tablespoon chopped parsley

PREPARATION

1. Preheat oven to 350°F.

2. In a medium bowl, whisk together the cream cheese, ricotta, egg, and spices until completely smooth. Set aside.

3. In a skillet, heat 1 tablespoon olive oil over medium-high heat. Add the shallot, garlic, red bell pepper, and mushrooms. Sauté for about 5 minutes until the veggies are soft and just beginning to brown. Remove from the heat.

4. Spread the ricotta mixture in a 9-inch pie dish. Top with the pizza sauce in an even layer. Sprinkle with half of the Parmesan cheese and all of the veggies. Top with the mozzarella cheese and the remaining Parmesan and the pepperoni slices.

5. Bake for 25 to 30 minutes, until hot and bubbly and the top is golden brown. Garnish with chopped parsley and enjoy.

spinach ARTICHOKE **dip**

when my best friend Kim and I get together we always eat our favorite recipes and Spinach Artichoke Dip is, without fail, at the top of the list. It's piping hot and delicious and all that spinach makes us feel like we're (sort of) eating something healthy.

Makes 8 to 12 servings

INGREDIENTS

1 tablespoon olive oil
1 (14-ounce) can artichoke hearts, drained and chopped
2 garlic cloves, minced
1 (6-ounce) package baby spinach leaves
1 cup mayonnaise
1 (8-ounce) package cream cheese, softened
1 cup grated Parmesan cheese
1 cup shredded mozzarella cheese
1 teaspoon salt
1 teaspoon black pepper
½ teaspoon Italian seasoning
1 cup croutons, crushed
Pita chips or crackers, for serving

PREPARATION

1. Preheat the oven to 375°F.

2. In a saucepan, heat 1 tablespoon of olive oil over medium-high heat. Add the artichokes, garlic, and spinach. Cook for 5 to 8 minutes until the spinach is wilted.

3. In a medium bowl, combine the mayonnaise, cream cheese, Parmesan cheese, and mozzarella cheese.

4. Add the mixture to the hot saucepan with the veggies and stir until melted and evenly combined. Season with salt, black pepper, and Italian seasoning. Pour the mixture into an 8- or 9-inch baking dish and top with the crushed croutons. Bake for about 15 minutes until bubbly and golden brown on top.

5. Serve warm with pita chips or crackers on the side.

spicy corn DIP

easily the most popular
dish on the chic site! xo

several years ago my friend Patty Fallahee graciously allowed me to share her recipe for Spicy Corn Dip on the Chic Site, and it's still one of our most popular posts. It's got a bit of heat from the chipotle, a crunch from the corn and peppers, and it's all wrapped inside melted cheesy goodness. A *must* try!

Makes 8 to 12 servings

INGREDIENTS

2 tablespoons butter
1 yellow onion, chopped
5 garlic cloves, minced
1 red bell pepper, chopped
3 cups corn (frozen or fresh)
1½ (8-ounce) packages cream cheese, softened
2 cups shredded Cheddar cheese
2 cups shredded Pepper Jack cheese
1½ cups mayonnaise
½ cup cilantro, chopped
1 large bunch scallions, chopped (about 1 cup)
2 tablespoons chipotle in adobo sauce (from chipotle pepper in adobo sauce can)
2 tablespoons hot sauce (or more if you like it super spicy)
½ teaspoon salt
½ teaspoon black pepper

PREPARATION

1. Preheat oven to 350°F.

2. In a large skillet, sauté the butter and the yellow onion, garlic, red bell pepper, and corn over medium heat until the onion is soft and translucent, about 5 minutes. Remove from the heat and stir in the cream cheese until combined.

3. In a large bowl, mix the remaining ingredients with the veggies and cream cheese mixture. Taste and adjust seasonings accordingly.

4. Pour the dip into an oven-safe baking dish. Bake for 20 to 25 minutes, or until the top is golden brown and the edges are bubbling.

5. Serve hot out of the oven with chips or chopped veggies. Enjoy!

we've all made seven-layer dip, right? A few years back I thought it would be fun to create a different version, and I came up with this! Hummus instead of beans, Greek yogurt instead of sour cream, feta instead of Cheddar. These dips are cousins all right, but the flavor palates are totally different. If you like Mediterranean flavors, you're going to love this.

//

Makes 8 to 12 servings

INGREDIENTS

1 (25-ounce) container plain hummus
1 cup of plain Greek yogurt
½ red onion, diced
5 sweet peppers, diced
¼ cup Greek-style kalamata olives, diced
¼ cup crumbled feta cheese
2 tablespoons pine nuts
1 teaspoon dried oregano
Cucumber slices, carrot sticks, green bell pepper slices, or pita chips, for serving

PREPARATION

1. Use a spatula to spread the bottom layer of your hummus on the plate or bowl you'll be using to serve your dip. I use a large plate, but you could do your dip in a bowl or casserole dish.

2. Then top with a layer of Greek yogurt. Since Greek yogurt is so thick, I put mine in a baggie and snip off a corner to use it like a pastry bag. It makes it easier to spread.

3. Top with the onion, peppers, and olives as their own separate layers.

4. Sprinkle the top with crumbled feta, pine nuts, and dried oregano.

5. Serve with cucumber slices, carrot sticks, green bell pepper slices, or pita chips for dipping.

greek
SEVEN-
LAYER
dip

grilled GUACAMOLE

this is such a cool twist on a classic appetizer! By grilling all of the ingredients—from the avocado to the onions–you add in a smoky flavor that enhances every part of this dish. Try it out the next time you're making Mexican food!

Makes 8 to 12 servings

INGREDIENTS

4 ripe avocados
3 small tomatoes
1 small red onion
2 jalapeños (optional)
2 limes
¼ cup cilantro, chopped
1 teaspoon salt
½ teaspoon black pepper
¼ teaspoon cumin
¼ teaspoon paprika

PREPARATION

1. Heat a stovetop or outdoor grill to medium-high and lightly grease with cooking spray or vegetable oil.

2. Cut the avocados in half, remove the pits, but keep the skin. Grill the avocados facedown for 2 to 3 minutes to develop grill marks. Transfer the avocados to a plate or platter. Cut the tomatoes in half, lengthwise, and grill for 2 to 3 minutes cut side down to char. Transfer the tomatoes to a plate. Cut the red onion into large rings. Keep the rings intact and grill for 2 to 3 minutes per side. Cut the jalapeños, if using, and limes in half and grill for 1 to 2 minutes.

3. Transfer the veggies and limes to a plate and allow to cool.

4. Cut the grilled veggies into chunks and throw them into a bowl. Mash everything together along with the chopped cilantro, seasonings, and the juice of the grilled limes, until completely combined.

5. Serve with chips or cut-up veggies. Enjoy!

casseroles

If recipes were high school students, I feel like the casserole would be the slightly overweight girl who wears braces and plays third-chair clarinet. And I adore her. Probably because I was that exact girl as a teenager, and I like to believe that people would've seen I was cool if they'd only given me a chance . . . just like casseroles. You take all of your favorite ingredients, mix them together in Pyrex, and bake them into something amazing. Casseroles are awesome for a potluck and the perfect dish to make for a new mama who doesn't have time to cook dinner. I mean, seriously, what's not to love? Okay, there's maybe one thing. Casseroles don't always look as pretty as they taste, but I'm about to change all of that. In this chapter, I really want to show you how gorgeous a casserole can be. Sometimes it means using an interesting baking dish. Sometimes it means adding a garnish to make the recipe pop. But I promise you can serve any of these casseroles at your next dinner party with pride.

CASSEROLES

breakfast
MONKEY bread

food bloggers follow trends just like anybody else, and there was a period of time a couple of years ago when everyone was covering monkey bread, trying to one up each other with their own cool spin on it. For weeks I wondered, how could I make a monkey bread that was different? And then it hit me in the middle of the night—seriously. Breakfast Monkey Bread! What if we stuffed biscuits with eggs and potatoes and cheese and breakfast meat and we served it with country gravy to dip? Just further proof that my best ideas come to me in my sleep.

Makes 6 to 8 servings

INGREDIENTS

6 large eggs
splash of milk
½ teaspoon of salt
¼ teaspoon of black pepper
8 slices bacon, cooked and chopped
2 cups tater tots, crisped in the oven
3 (16.3-ounce) cans biscuits
3 tablespoons butter, melted
1 cup shredded Cheddar or Monterey Jack cheese

For the gravy:
1 tablespoon butter
1 cup cooked turkey sausage, crumbled
3 tablespoons flour
1½ cups whole milk
½ teaspoon salt
½ teaspoon black pepper

PREPARATION

1. Preheat the oven to 350°F. Grease a Bundt or tube pan and set aside.

2. In a bowl, whisk the eggs with a splash of milk, and half the salt and pepper. In a skillet, scramble the eggs over medium heat until cooked through, about 10 minutes. Add the crisped bacon and tater tots. Allow to cool slightly.

3. Cut the biscuits in half (or quarters if you want smaller pieces) and fill them with a bit of the egg filling. Form into a ball and place into the prepared pan. Stack them on top of each other, brushing each layer of rolled dough with melted butter, and sprinkle with cheese. Bake for 20 to 25 minutes or until golden brown and cooked through. Allow to cool for 5 minutes before inverting onto a plate.

4. To make the gravy: in a small pot, melt a tablespoon of butter over medium-high heat. Add the sausage and heat through. Add the flour, stirring, and cook for a few seconds.

5. Whisk in the milk and cook until the mixture has thickened. Season with remaining salt and pepper. Serve alongside the monkey bread as a dipping sauce.

tamale PIE

my husband and i have a lot of things in common, and a longstanding relationship with tamale pie is one of them. Growing up, we both saw this dish on the dinner table in our homes at least once a week. It has a base of ground beef, spices, peppers, black olives, and cheese topped with corn bread, then baked. It's easy and kids love it, so it's no wonder both our moms were such big fans.

//

Makes 4 to 6 servings

INGREDIENTS

2 pounds ground beef
2 large poblano peppers, diced
1 cup frozen corn
1 (7-ounce) can sliced black olives, drained
1 teaspoon salt
1 teaspoon chili powder
½ teaspoon dried oregano
1 (16-ounce) jar salsa
2 (8.5-ounce) boxes dry corn muffin mix
2 large eggs
⅔ cup milk
½ cup shredded Cheddar cheese
½ cup shredded Monterey Jack cheese

PREPARATION

1. Preheat the oven to 350°F.

2. In a large cast-iron skillet, cook and stir the ground beef over medium-high heat until the meat starts to brown and release its juices, about 5 minutes. Add in the poblano peppers, corn, olives, salt, chili powder, and oregano. Stir to evenly combine and cook for another 10 minutes. Stir in the salsa and remove from the heat.

3. In a large bowl, mix both packages of dry corn muffin mix with the eggs and milk. Stir until the batter is smooth and lump-free.

4. Pour the batter over the seasoned beef, spreading it in an even layer. Top with the cheeses and bake for 50 to 60 minutes until golden brown, or until a toothpick inserted in the corn bread layer comes out clean.

why meat loaf? why not

meat loaf? is the better question. I'm convinced that people who don't like meat loaf just haven't had a good version yet. This recipe is made with mushrooms and balsamic, and then the whole loaf is wrapped in bacon. It's wrapped in bacon, people! If that won't convince you to try it, nothing will.

Makes 4 to 6 servings

INGREDIENTS

2 pounds ground beef
1 packet onion soup mix (such as Lipton's)
½ yellow onion, minced (about ½ cup)
1 cup button mushrooms, chopped
3 tablespoons balsamic vinegar
1 large egg, lightly beaten
8 to 10 slices bacon

PREPARATION

1. Preheat the oven to 350°F. Line a baking sheet with aluminum foil, grease lightly with cooking spray, and set aside.

2. In a large bowl, mix together all of the ingredients (except the bacon) until well combined. Do not overmix.

3. Shape the mixture into a ball and transfer to the prepared baking sheet. Using your hands, form the mixture into a loaf. Cover the top with the bacon slices, tucking the ends of the slices underneath the meat loaf. Cook for 45 minutes to 1 hour or until golden brown and crispy all around and fully cooked through the center. Remove from the oven and allow to cool down slightly before cutting and serving.

if you want to drizzle a little extra balsamic over the top before you cook it, well, that wouldn't hurt my feelings one bit! xo

balsamic
bacon-wrapped
MEAT LOAF

this works great with
ground turkey, too. xo

HAMBURGER
pot pie

when i was growing up, our family had pot pie at least one night a week. This is not that recipe. It's not that recipe because my parents were huge fans of the frozen pot pie . . . and who could blame them? A Swanson's pot pie with a slice of cheese melted on top is delicious. Unfortunately for me, my publisher would surely frown upon a recipe that's just directions for warming up a frozen dinner. So I came up with a whole new homemade hamburger pot pie that never once uses a microwave.

Makes 4 to 6 servings

INGREDIENTS

1 (14-ounce) package refrigerated pie crust (2 crusts) at room temperature
2 pounds ground beef
1 yellow onion, diced
2 garlic cloves, minced
2 celery stalks, diced
1 (12-ounce) package frozen veggies (corn, peas, green beans, and carrots), thawed
1 (14-ounce) can diced tomatoes
1 teaspoon salt
½ teaspoon black pepper
1 large egg, whisked with a splash of water
½ teaspoon fresh rosemary, chopped

PREPARATION

1. Preheat the oven to 400°F. Line the bottom of a 9-inch pie dish with 1 pie crust. Trim the excess crust and set aside.

2. In a large pot, cook the ground beef over medium-high heat until browned, about 10 minutes. Stir in the onion, garlic, celery, and frozen veggies. Cook until the veggies are softened and warmed through, about 5 minutes. Add the tomatoes, salt, and black pepper and cook for another minute or two. Allow to cool slightly.

3. Pour the beef filling into the prepared pie dish.

4. Top with the second crust and crimp the edges of the top and bottom crusts together. Using a sharp knife, cut a few slits in the top to allow steam to escape.

5. Brush with the egg wash and sprinkle with rosemary and a pinch of salt and pepper. Bake for about 35 minutes or until the crust is golden brown.

BACON
and
green
chile
MAC 'n'
cheese

mac 'n' cheese is one of those recipes I've spent most of my adult life perfecting. I started with an old recipe and every time I made it, I'd add a bit more cayenne or a tad more garlic. While it was always good, it wasn't spectacular . . . and if you're going to make homemade mac 'n' cheese you want it to be spectacular, right? Then one fateful day, I happened to have some leftover green chiles and I threw them into the mix. Holy smokes, you guys, green chiles are everything! This recipe is cheesy and creamy with just a touch of heat. You're gonna love it.

Makes 6 to 8 servings

INGREDIENTS

1 tablespoon olive oil
1 yellow onion, chopped
3 garlic cloves, minced
1 tablespoon + 1 teaspoon salt
1 pound macaroni (or any other short-cut pasta)
4 tablespoons unsalted butter, divided
3 tablespoons all-purpose flour
1½ cups whole milk, warmed
½ teaspoon freshly ground black pepper
1 teaspoon cayenne pepper
1¼ cups grated sharp Cheddar cheese, divided
1¼ cups grated Monterey Jack cheese, divided
1 (4-ounce) can diced green chiles
1 pound bacon, diced and cooked until crispy
½ cup plain bread crumbs

PREPARATION

1. Preheat the oven to 350°F. In a large skillet, warm the olive oil over medium-high heat. Add the onion and garlic until the onion just begins to caramelize, about 5 minutes. Remove from the heat and set aside. Bring a large pot of water to a boil and season with 1 tablespoon of salt. Add the dried pasta and cook until al dente according to package's instructions. You don't want to overcook the noodles, as they'll continue to cook in the oven. Drain and set aside.

2. Warm a medium saucepan and melt 3 tablespoons of butter over medium-high heat. Add the flour and stir to evenly combine. Cook for a few seconds and then whisk in the warmed milk, making sure the flour and butter have dissolved. Season with remaining salt, black pepper, and cayenne and simmer until bubbly and thick. Remove from the heat and stir in 1 cup Cheddar and 1 cup Monterey Jack cheese.

3. Add the green chiles and the crispy bacon (saving some bacon for the topping). Add in the cooked noodles and onion and garlic and stir until evenly combined.

4. Generously grease a baking dish with 1 tablespoon butter—this keeps the macaroni from sticking once it's baked. Pour the mac 'n' cheese in the baking dish and top with the remaining cheeses and reserved bacon. Bake for 20 to 25 minutes or until bubbly and the top is golden brown.

this is my mother-in-law

Patty's famous dish. She brings it to every holiday and most parties regardless of the time of year because everyone loves it. Since it's so good, she typically has to make two pans and there are still rarely any leftovers. This is a classic casserole and probably has a "real" name, but it will forever be known as Patty Potatoes to the Hollis clan.

Makes 6 to 8 servings

INGREDIENTS

¼ pound (1 stick) unsalted butter or margarine
2 (10.75-ounce) cans cream of chicken soup
1 pint sour cream
2 cups grated Cheddar cheese
6 scallions, sliced (about ¾ cup)
2 pounds frozen hash brown potatoes, thawed

PREPARATION

1. Preheat the oven to 350°F.

2. In a large pot, melt the butter over medium-high heat and stir in the soup until well combined.

3. Mix in the sour cream, cheese, and scallions (reserving a little bit of cheese and scallions for the top).

4. Fold in the potatoes until evenly incorporated.

5. Pour the mixture into a casserole dish, spreading in an even layer. Top with the reserved cheese and scallions and bake for 40 to 45 minutes until bubbly and golden brown. Serve warm.

want to knock it out of the park?
mix in some bacon! xo

patty
potatoes

corn
muffin
CASSEROLE

serve a scoop of this with
the turkey chili, on page 105. xo

this is another one of my mother-in-law's go-to recipes. She started making this corn muffin casserole ages ago and bringing it to potlucks along with her potatoes. It's a bit like cornbread, but sweeter and not as dense. I love making it to go along with a big pot of chili or beef stew.

Makes 6 to 8 servings

INGREDIENTS

1 box corn muffin mix (such as Jiffy)
1 (15-ounce) can creamed corn
Kernels from 2 ears fresh corn (about 1 cup), washed
1 large egg
4 tablespoons (½ stick) butter, melted

PREPARATION

1. Preheat the oven to 350°F. Lightly grease an 8- or 9-inch baking dish with cooking spray or butter, set aside.

2. In a bowl, combine all of the ingredients until evenly incorporated.

3. Pour the mixture into baking dish and bake for 20 to 25 minutes or until a toothpick inserted in the middle comes out clean.

4. Place under the broiler for the last few minutes to brown the top. Remove from the oven and allow to cool slightly before serving.

GREEN
chicken
ENCHILADAS

this is a recipe that could easily be a total pain to make. Some people might make the green sauce from scratch and sauté fresh chicken in lime juice. Me? I use every trick in the book to make this as simple as possible, using store-bought green enchilada sauce and some sour cream to balance out the heat. The end result is just as pretty and delicious as one that might take you hours to prep.

Makes 4 to 6 servings

INGREDIENTS

1 (19-ounce) can green enchilada sauce
1 cup sour cream
1 tablespoon olive oil
3 chicken breasts, cut into 1-inch strips
1 yellow onion, sliced
1 packet taco seasoning mix
Juice of 1 lime
12 corn tortillas
2 cups shredded Monterey Jack cheese

PREPARATION

1. Preheat the oven to 350°F.

2. In a medium bowl, whisk the enchilada sauce and sour cream until smooth. Pour half of it into a 9 by 13-inch baking dish and set aside. Reserve the remaining sauce for later.

3. In a large skillet, heat the oil over medium-high heat. Once hot, add the chicken and sauté until golden brown and crispy, about 10 minutes. Stir in the onion and cook for another 3 to 5 minutes to soften. Add the taco seasoning mix and lime juice and stir until combined. Remove from the heat and allow the chicken to cool slightly.

4. In a dry skillet, warm a tortilla over medium heat to make it pliable. Off heat, fill the tortilla with the chicken mixture and shredded cheese. Roll into a log and place in the prepared baking dish. Repeat with the remaining tortillas until all are filled and rolled, reserving some cheese for the topping.

5. Spoon the reserved sauce over the enchiladas and top with the remaining cheese. Bake for 20 to 25 minutes until warmed through and the cheese has melted.

fine. this recipe isn't my aunt Linda's, it's mine. However, I associate all tuna casseroles with my aunt Linda because she's the only one who made them when I was growing up. I know that most often this is made with canned goods, but trust me, adding a few fresh ingredients is going to make this the best tuna casserole you've ever had.

Makes 4 to 6 servings

INGREDIENTS

1 (10.5 ounce) can cream of mushroom soup
½ cup whole milk
1 cup frozen peas, thawed
2 (5-ounce) cans tuna in water, drained
1 tablespoon fresh dill
1 tablespoon fresh lemon juice
4 ounces (about 2 cups) egg noodles, cooked and drained
¼ cup plain bread crumbs
2 tablespoons unsalted butter, melted

PREPARATION

1. Preheat the oven to 400°F. Lightly grease a 1½-quart casserole dish and set aside.

2. In a bowl, mix the soup, milk, peas, tuna, dill, and lemon juice until well combined. Stir in the egg noodles. Pour the mixture into the prepared casserole dish.

3. In a small bowl, toss together the bread crumbs and melted butter.

4. Sprinkle on top of the casserole and bake for 20 to 25 minutes until golden brown and bubbly.

if fresh peas are in season, use them instead of frozen for an even brighter flavor. xo

aunt linda's
TUNA
casserole

supreme
PIZZA
pasta
bake

every friday, the hollis family orders pizza. We've done it for as long as I can remember, and my boys look forward to it all week long. This pasta dish combines the pizza flavors we love in casserole form, and the best part is you can make any flavor pasta you like by substituting your favorite pizza toppings.

//

Makes 4 to 6 servings

INGREDIENTS

1 tablespoon olive oil
1 red onion, sliced
1 green bell pepper, sliced
1 pound crimini mushrooms, sliced
1 tablespoon + 1 teaspoon salt
1 pound pasta
1 (2.25-ounce) can sliced black olives, drained
1 (14-ounce) jar pizza sauce
1 (15-ounce) container ricotta cheese
½ teaspoon freshly cracked black pepper
2 cups shredded mozzarella cheese, divided
16 slices pepperoni, divided
Fresh parsley, chopped, for garnish

PREPARATION

1. Preheat the oven to 350°F.

2. In a large skillet, heat the olive oil over medium-high heat. Once hot, add the onion, bell pepper, and mushrooms. Cook for 5 to 8 minutes or until the onion is soft and just beginning to caramelize. Remove from the heat and set aside.

3. Bring a large pot of cold water to a boil. Season with 1 tablespoon of salt and throw in the pasta. Cook according to package directions until al dente. Drain and transfer the pasta to a large mixing bowl.

4. In a large bowl or pot, toss the cooked noodles, sautéed veggies, black olives, pizza sauce, ricotta, remaining salt, and black pepper.

5. Pour half of the mixture into a 9 by 13-inch baking dish. Top with half of the mozzarella cheese and half of the pepperoni. Pour the remainder of the pasta on top and top with the rest of the mozzarella and pepperoni. Bake for 20 to 25 minutes or until bubbly and golden brown. Garnish with a bit of chopped fresh parsley and serve immediately.

slow cooker

When I was growing up, I only remember my mama ever making two things in her slow cooker. Pot roast, which I loved, and pinto beans, which I hated with the burning intensity of a thousand suns. Luckily for me, as an adult, I figured out that you can make just about anything inside a slow cooker and the results can be way more delicious than Mama's beans. On the Chic Site, slow cooker recipes are our most popular category, hands down. I think the reason ours go over so well (besides being tasty) is that we show them off beautifully rather than leaving them inside the pot. Because here's the secret, guys—these can be some of the greatest recipes in your arsenal for entertaining. You just have to put them into a pretty new container to serve them.

SLOW COOKER

you can mix the rice
in but I serve it on top
because it's prettier. xo

JAMBALAYA

my mom's side of the family *loves* spicy food, so it's no wonder jambalaya has been part of her repertoire for as long as I can remember. Sausage, shrimp, rice, peppers, and spices work together in this recipe to create an incredible meal. The best part? The leftovers are delicious! I've been known to polish off a whole pot all by myself.

Makes 6 to 8 servings

INGREDIENTS

1 tablespoon salted butter
1 pound chicken breast, cut into 2-inch chunks
3 stalks celery, chopped
1 bell pepper, chopped
1 medium onion, chopped
⅛ to ¼ teaspoon cayenne pepper
2 teaspoons Creole or Cajun seasoning
1 tablespoon tomato paste
1 (28-ounce) can diced tomatoes
2 cups reduced-sodium chicken broth
12 ounces Cajun-style andouille pork sausage, sliced
2½ cups long-grain rice
12 ounces frozen cooked shrimp
Parsley, for topping
Salt and black pepper

PREPARATION

1. In a large skillet, melt the butter on medium-high heat. Sear the chicken on all sides. No need to fully cook the chicken, just sear to get some color. Transfer the chicken to a clean bowl. Add the celery, bell pepper, and onion to the skillet. Cook until the onion begins to soften. Add cayenne pepper, Cajun seasoning, and tomato paste, and mix. Remove from the heat.

2. In the slow cooker, add the diced tomatoes (along with juice) and chicken broth. Add the seared chicken and sliced sausage. Follow with the celery-onion mixture. Cover the slow cooker and cook for 4 to 6 hours on the medium setting. If you're using uncooked rice, add the rice to the slow cooker in the last 30 minutes of cooking. Cover and cook for 30 minutes on the high setting. If you're using cooked rice, add the rice after the shrimp has warmed.

3. Once the rice is cooked, add the frozen shrimp. Cover the slow cooker and cook the shrimp until warm, for 8 to 10 minutes. Serve warm and garnish with parsley and additional Cajun seasoning as needed. Add salt and pepper to taste.

this has always been a favorite of all my mama's dishes, and it's still the thing I crave most if I'm sick. I have a lifetime of memories wrapped up in this simple recipe, but none so special as the time period after my boys were born. My mom held my hand (and my husband's, too) as I went through the labor for each one of our children. Afterward, when I came home from the hospital excited and exhausted and overwhelmed, my mom had a big pot of Chicken 'n' Dumplings simmering on the stove for me. I think, with the first baby, I probably ate the entire pot by myself.

Makes 4 to 6 servings

INGREDIENTS

1 yellow onion, diced
2 medium carrots, peeled and diced
2 large celery stalks, diced
2 garlic cloves, minced
1 rotisserie chicken, skinned and shredded
4 cups chicken stock
2 (10.5-ounce) cans cream of chicken soup
2 teaspoons garlic salt
½ teaspoon black pepper
½ teaspoon dried thyme
½ teaspoon dried oregano
¼ teaspoon paprika
2 cups Bisquick baking mix
⅔ cup milk
½ cup (6-8 slices) crispy bacon, chopped
3 tablespoons chives, chopped

PREPARATION

1. Combine all of the ingredients (except for the baking mix, milk, bacon, and chives) in the bowl of the slow cooker.

2. Cook on low for 6 to 8 hours or on high for 3 to 4 hours.

3. About 30 minutes before serving, in a large bowl, combine the baking mix with the milk. Drop the biscuits by the spoonful into the slow cooker. Cook until the dough is no longer raw in the center (about half an hour). Serve with a sprinkling of crumbled bacon and fresh chives.

chicken 'n' DUMPLINGS

mango-
CHIPOTLE
carnitas

be sure to really wash your hands after dicing that pepper so you don't accidentally rub your eye with pepper fingers. ouch! xo *i love making any kind* of shredded meat in a slow cooker. That's kind of a weird thing to proclaim my love for, but it's true. I feel like anytime I try something shredded in the oven I accidentally dry it out. But in the slow cooker, I'm a shredded-meat all-star, and the meat always comes out moist. These carnitas have so much flavor and turn into the best tacos you'll ever have.

Makes 8 to 12 servings

INGREDIENTS

3 to 4 pounds pork shoulder
2 teaspoons salt, divided
1 teaspoon black pepper
1 teaspoon chili powder
½ white onion, diced
1 jalapeño, seeded and diced
1 (28-ounce) can mango slices
2 large oranges
1 lime
¾ cup chicken stock
2 chipotle peppers in adobo sauce (from a can)

PREPARATION

1. Season all sides of the pork shoulder with 1 teaspoon salt, black pepper, and chili powder. Place the pork in the slow cooker and cover with the diced onion and jalapeño. Remove two sections of mango from the can (reserving the juice). The mango is very mushy, so I mash it over the top of the pork so it absorbs the flavor.

2. In a separate bowl, combine all of the mango juice from your can with the juice of the two oranges, the juice of the lime, and the chicken stock. Mix well. Dice two of the chipotle peppers and add to your juice mixture and mix well. Pour juice mixture over the pork and season again with remaining salt. Cover and cook 8 hours on low or 4 hours on high.

3. Once cooked, carefully remove the pork from the slow cooker and transfer to a cutting board. Using a knife and fork, shred or chop the pork into smaller pieces. Return the pork to the sauce and keep warm until ready to serve.

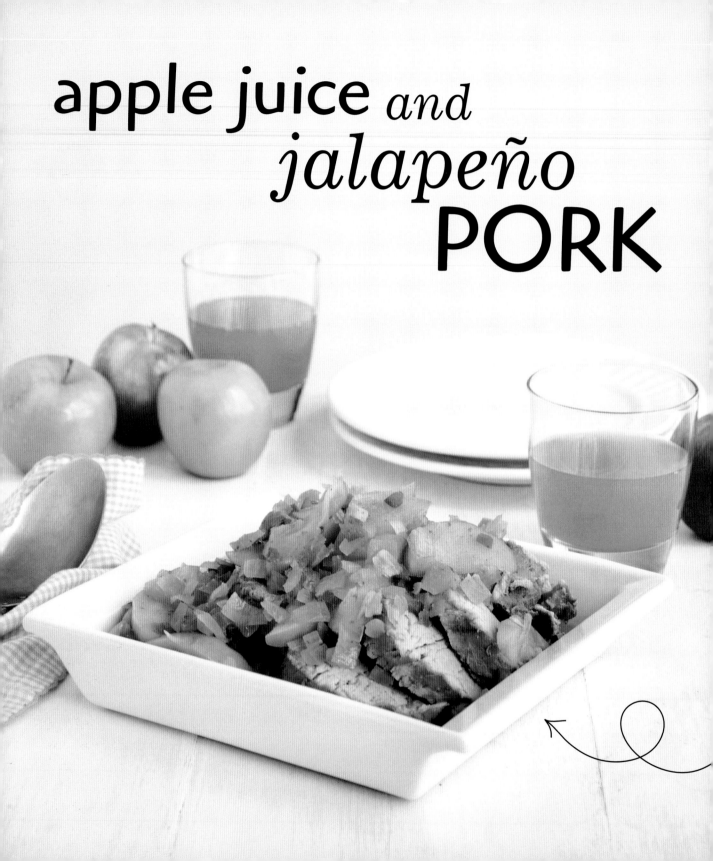

apple juice *and* jalapeño PORK

i was having dinner with some friends in Utah years ago and our host mentioned an incredible recipe he had for an apple juice and jalapeño glaze. He was so excited by the combination, I knew I had to try to make it myself. Guys, it's pork-tastic and applicious! You've got to give this one a try.

Makes 6 to 8 servings

INGREDIENTS

2½ pounds pork tenderloin
1½ teaspoons salt
1 teaspoon black pepper
2 tablespoons salted butter, melted
1 medium sweet onion, chopped
3 jalapeño peppers, seeded and chopped
2 cups chicken stock
1 can frozen apple juice concentrate, thawed
3 tablespoons light brown sugar
2 apples, cored and sliced

PREPARATION

1. Season the pork tenderloin with the salt and black pepper.

2. Place the pork in the bowl of the slow cooker and cover with the remaining ingredients except the apples. Cook on low for 6 to 8 hours or on high for 3 to 4 hours.

3. Halfway through cooking, stir in the sliced apples and continue cooking for the remaining time. Cut or break apart the pork with two forks and serve with the sauce spooned over.

serve this with
the accordion
potatoes on 134. xo

TURKEY *chili*

this was one of the first dishes I mastered as a newlywed. When I say I mastered it, I mean that I finally figured out the right blend of spices and ingredients necessary to make it delicious. I like to make a big pot on Sunday so that we can eat it throughout the week. As with all chili, the flavor gets better with every passing day.

Makes 6 to 8 servings

INGREDIENTS

1 tablespoon olive oil
2 pounds ground turkey
1 large yellow onion, diced
3 garlic cloves, minced
1 tablespoon garlic salt
2 tablespoons chili powder
¼ teaspoon black pepper
3 (14-ounce) cans diced tomatoes
1 (14-ounce) can red kidney beans, drained and rinsed
1 (14-ounce) can black beans, drained and rinsed
1 (14-ounce) can pinto beans, drained and rinsed
1 (8-ounce) can tomato sauce
2 cups corn kernels, fresh or frozen
1 (4-ounce) can diced green chiles (optional)

PREPARATION

1. Heat a large skillet over medium-high heat and drizzle in the oil. Once hot, add the ground turkey and cook, breaking the meat up with a wooden spoon until browned and crispy, 5 to 7 minutes.

2. Add the onion, garlic, garlic salt, chili powder, and black pepper to the meat. Mix to evenly combine. Cook for about 3 minutes or until the onion has softened.

3. In the bowl of a slow cooker, combine the cooked turkey mixture, diced tomatoes, beans, tomato sauce, corn, and green chiles, if using. Stir to fully incorporate.

4. Cover and cook on low for 6 to 8 hours or on high for 2 to 4 hours.

5. I like to serve the chili with little bowls of sour cream, cheese, chips, scallions, guacamole, and salsa so guests can top their chili however they'd like.

my uncle joe loved to cook

and bake and then get together with the family to eat what he'd made. I have the sweetest memories of the two of us baking half-moon pies at his home in Northern California and of winter weekends enjoying this soup with him in Grandma Opal's kitchen. I honestly think he just threw anything they had on hand into a pot and let it bubble and simmer into something wonderful. Follow this recipe as a base, but feel free to make like Uncle Joe and add anything you'd like to the mix.

Makes 6 to 8 servings

INGREDIENTS

2 pounds ground sirloin or ground beef
1 large yellow onion, chopped
3 garlic cloves, chopped
1 teaspoon salt
1 teaspoon black pepper
½ teaspoon cumin
½ teaspoon paprika
3 tablespoons tomato paste
1 yellow bell pepper, diced
1 red bell pepper, diced
1 green bell pepper, diced
2 stalks celery, diced
2 large carrots, peeled and diced
6 red potatoes, diced
1 (14.5-ounce) can diced tomatoes
4 cups beef stock
Saltine crackers, for topping

PREPARATION

1. Heat a sauté pan over medium-high heat. Cook the ground sirloin, breaking the meat up with a wooden spoon, until brown and crispy. Add the diced onion and garlic. Season with salt, black pepper, cumin, and paprika, and cook for about 5 minutes.

2. Add the tomato paste and mix with the meat. Place the meat mixture in the slow cooker. Add in the remaining veggies, canned tomatoes, and beef stock. Cook on low for 6 to 8 hours or on high for 3 to 4 hours.

3. I like to serve mine with saltine crackers on the side.

uncle joe's
hamburger
STEW

BBQ *baked* BEANS

baked beans are a classic side dish for cookouts and grilling. I'm typically so busy prepping all the other food that I have a bad habit of just using some canned baked beans and calling it good. But with this recipe I've got no excuse. I throw the beans in early in the day and by the time the burgers come off the grill, they're ready to serve.

Makes 6 to 8 servings

INGREDIENTS

8 slices bacon, diced
1 yellow onion, diced
1 green bell pepper, diced
1 jalapeño, chopped (optional)
4 (15-ounce) cans navy beans
½ cup light brown sugar
1 cup barbecue sauce
2 tablespoons ketchup
1 tablespoon Dijon mustard
¼ cup maple syrup
1 tablespoon apple cider vinegar
3 tablespoons bourbon (optional)
1 teaspoon garlic powder
1 teaspoon cracked black pepper

PREPARATION

1. In a skillet, cook the bacon over medium-high heat until crispy, about 7 minutes. Transfer to a plate lined with paper towels. Discard most of the grease, leaving about 1 tablespoon in the skillet.

2. Cook the onion, green bell pepper, and jalapeño (if using) in the skillet over medium-high heat, stirring frequently, until soft, about 10 minutes.

3. Drain and rinse the beans in a colander, reserving two of the cans' liquid. Place the beans, reserved liquid, cooked bacon, sautéed vegetables, and the rest of the ingredients in the slow cooker.

4. Stir until completely combined. Cook on low for about 4 hours or on high for about 2 hours. Eat while hot.

i love anytime you can throw a handful of ingredients in a pot and come home hours later to something delicious. And, guys, I know root beer might seem like an odd choice for a savory dish, but it adds some really great flavor to the poultry and makes your house smell like a summer barbecue while it cooks.

Makes 6 to 8 servings

INGREDIENTS

4 to 5 pounds bone-in chicken legs
1 teaspoon salt
½ teaspoon black pepper
1 (16-ounce) bottle root beer
1 (17-ounce) bottle barbecue sauce

PREPARATION

1. Place the chicken in the slow cooker and season with the salt and black pepper. Cover and cook on high for 1½ hours.

2. In a small bowl, mix the root beer and barbecue sauce. Pour the sauce over the chicken and cover again.

3. Cook for another 1½ hours, until tender and falling apart.

this works on chicken breasts and thighs as well. xo

BBQ
root beer
chicken

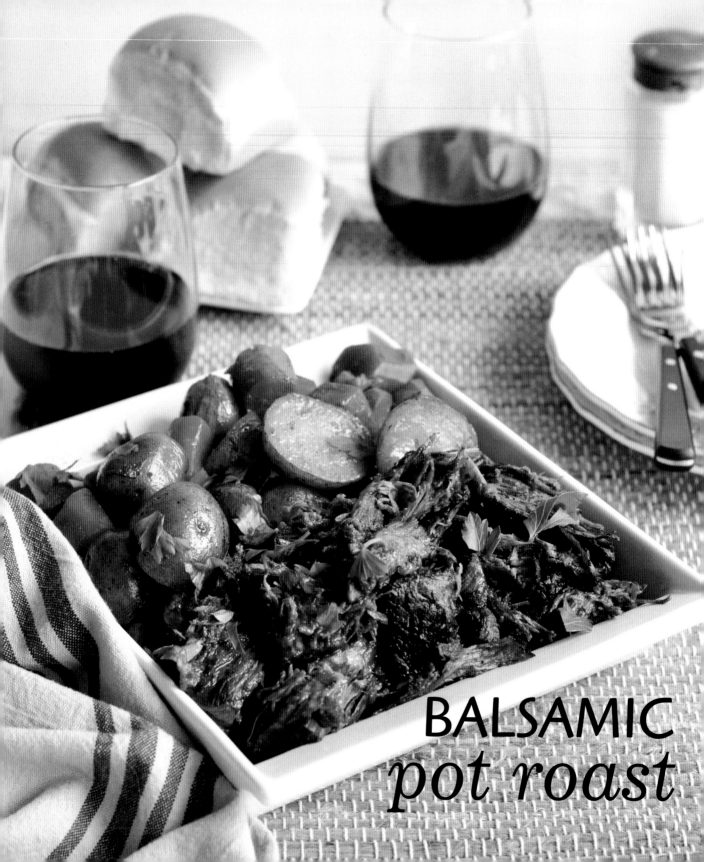

BALSAMIC
pot roast

to date, i think this recipe has brought over half a million visitors to my Web site. It's so simple to make, but the flavor the balsamic and the citrus add to the roast will absolutely blow your mind. It's on regular rotation as a dinner option in our home and if you haven't tried it yet, you should absolutely include it as part of your next Sunday supper.

Makes 4 to 6 servings

INGREDIENTS

4 to 5 pounds beef chuck roast
½ pound baby red potatoes, quartered
2 medium carrots, peeled and cut into large chunks
2 cups beef broth
½ cup light brown sugar
¼ cup balsamic vinegar
1 tablespoon soy sauce
1 teaspoon salt
¼ teaspoon crushed red pepper flakes
3 cloves garlic, minced
1 tablespoon fresh orange zest

PREPARATION

1. Place meat, potatoes, and carrots into the slow cooker.

2. In a medium bowl, whisk together all the other ingredients and pour over the top of the meat.

3. Cook on low for 6 to 8 hours or on high for 3 to 4 hours until tender.

use these flavorful potatoes to make mashed potatoes. . .you won't believe how good they are! xo

they say necessity is the mother of invention. Well, sometimes needing to use up the leftover chicken is the mother of invention, too. Years ago I had a rotisserie chicken and wasn't sure what to make, so I looked in my pantry. The pantry had enchilada sauce and beans and corn, and I thought, *Maybe I could make some kind of enchilada soup.* This one is a little spicy and so good.

Makes 6 to 8 servings

INGREDIENTS

4 (4–6oz) shredded cooked chicken breasts
1 (28-ounce) can mild green enchilada sauce
2 (14-ounce) cans low-sodium chicken broth
1 (14-ounce) can diced tomatoes w/ green chiles
1 (14-ounce) can black beans, drained and rinsed
1 cup frozen corn, thawed
1 onion, diced
2 garlic cloves, minced
1 large carrot, peeled and diced
Juice from 1 large lime (about 2 tablespoons)
½ tablespoon cumin
2 cups brown rice, cooked
Avocado, sour cream, Cheddar cheese, cilantro for topping

PREPARATION

1. Combine all of the ingredients except the rice and toppings in the bowl of a slow cooker.

2. Cook on high for 3 to 4 hours or on low for 6 to 8 hours. Everything is cooked already, but you want it to simmer and develop all of its flavor.

3. Serve with a scoop of brown rice and a topping of avocado, sour cream, cheese, and cilantro.

vegetarian? add an extra can of beans and substitute vegetable for chicken stock. it's just as delicious! xo

enchilada
SOUP

I framed dave's grandma's
kitchen utensils as wall decor

all my plates and
platters are inexpensive
and collected over time

the skirt is fancy,
the top is from target

potluck

I am a preacher's daughter, so potlucks are my jam. Potlucks were always such a big part of our church culture, but it was also a big part of my family's culture. A potluck alleviates the pressure on the host both physically and financially, and it's an opportunity for everyone to show off their best dish. Another major bonus is getting a plate filled with eighty-seven different foods. You know what I mean, right? If I'm going to blow my diet, I don't want to do it with a couple of extra cookies. . . . I want to do it with a potluck and a single plate that's the caloric equivalent of the entire Taco Bell menu. This chapter is a collection of my all-time favorite potluck recipes. Sadly, the Nacho Bell Grande didn't make the cut.

POTLUCK

fresh
GREEN
bean
salad

this is a great side dish for the
bbq root beer chicken on pg. 110. xo

what is it about a little

crunch in my food that makes me feel like something is healthy . . . even if it's tossed in buttermilk ranch dressing? All the summer produce makes this dish so vibrant and tasty, and the bacon and buttermilk mean that even veggie haters will love it, too.

//

Makes 4 to 6 servings

INGREDIENTS

1 pound fresh green beans, trimmed and cut in half
3 teaspoons salt, divided
1 cup mayonnaise
1 cup buttermilk
1 (16-ounce) package buttermilk ranch mix
1 cup cherry tomatoes, cut in half
Kernels cut from 2 ears fresh corn (about 1 cup), washed
8 slices bacon, chopped and cooked until crispy
Freshly cracked black pepper

PREPARATION

1. Bring a large pot of water to a boil. Season with a few teaspoons of salt and throw in the green bean pieces. Cook for about 5 minutes or until the green beans are tender and bright green.

2. Drain the green beans and transfer them to a bowl of ice water to stop the cooking and keep the bright green color. Drain and transfer to a bowl.

3. In a small bowl, combine the mayonnaise, buttermilk, and ranch mix.

4. Add the green beans to the cherry tomato halves, corn, bacon, and ranch dressing, and mix until combined. Season with a pinch of salt and a few grinds of freshly cracked black pepper.

5. Store the salad in the fridge until ready to serve. Allowing the salad to sit for at least a half hour will give it a chance to develop its flavors. Serve chilled.

i love this for a potluck

because it's more exciting than the average side salad. The flavors are great and each ingredient works together to create a crunchy, tangy dish that's perfect for any party. Bring along some paper takeout containers and chopsticks to eat this with, instead of paper plates. That's worth at least 100 cool points.

Makes 8 to 12 servings

INGREDIENTS

1 tablespoon olive oil
2 pounds chicken breast fillets
1 teaspoon salt
½ teaspoon black pepper
¼ teaspoon crushed red pepper flakes
1 bag shredded lettuce, cabbage, and carrot mix
½ cup sliced almonds
½ cup crispy wonton strips
3 scallions, sliced (about ¼ cup)
2 tablespoons sesame seeds
½ cup Asian vinaigrette

PREPARATION

1. In a large skillet, heat the oil over medium-high heat. In a large bowl, combine the chicken, salt, black pepper, and red pepper flakes. Add the chicken to the skillet and cook for 4 to 6 minutes, flip over, and cook for another 2 to 3 minutes. Remove the chicken from the heat and allow to rest for about 10 minutes before slicing.

2. In a large bowl, toss all of the remaining ingredients, along with the sliced chicken, with as much of the dressing as you'd like. Serve immediately.

my boys love to try eating with chopsticks. I just grab a few extras when we have takeout chinese food so we always have a supply. xo

chinese
chicken SALAD

loaded BAKED potato salad

any food without much color looks so much prettier in a colorful bowl or platter. xo *there are two kinds of people* in this world: macaroni salad people and potato salad people. I am a potato salad person. I love it in any form—old-school with mustard and pickles, fancy-style with fresh dill and red potatoes, or this, my favorite, loaded down like your favorite baked potato with all the fixings.

Makes 8 to 10 servings

INGREDIENTS

2 pounds baby Yukon gold potatoes, quartered
8 slices bacon, chopped and cooked until crispy
1 cup shredded sharp Cheddar cheese
½ cup mayonnaise
½ cup sour cream
5 scallions, chopped (about ½ cup)
1 teaspoon garlic salt
1 teaspoon seasoned salt

PREPARATION

1. Place the quartered potatoes in a pot and cover them with cold water. Bring to a boil over medium-high heat and cook until fork tender, 15 to 20 minutes.

2. Drain and allow the potatoes to cool completely.

3. Transfer the cooled potatoes to a large mixing bowl and add the cooked bacon, cheese, mayonnaise, sour cream, scallions, garlic salt, and seasoned salt. Toss to fully combine.

4. Cover and place in the fridge for at least 30 minutes to chill. If you have time, make a day ahead so the flavors can develop overnight. Serve chilled.

ambrosia

depending on where you grew up, you might call this something else. At Chic HQ some people called it "fluff," and a friend of mine swears they referred to it as "the pink stuff." I grew up calling it ambrosia—a mix of marshmallows, fruit, Cool Whip, Jell-O, and anything else we could think of to throw in. By serving it in individual portions instead of one large bowl, we're really elevating this classic dish—even if we can't agree on its name.

//

Makes 4 to 6 servings

INGREDIENTS

1 (8-ounce) container Cool Whip
½ cup vanilla Greek yogurt
1 cup shredded sweetened coconut
1 (11-ounce) can mandarin orange slices, drained
1 (8-ounce) can crushed pineapple
1 cup maraschino cherries, drained
½ cup pecans, chopped
2 cups mini multicolored marshmallows
Cool Whip, for topping
Maraschino cherries, for topping

PREPARATION

1. In a large bowl, mix the Cool Whip and vanilla yogurt until smooth.

2. Fold in the coconut, orange slices, pineapple, cherries, pecans, and marshmallows until evenly combined.

3. Spoon the ambrosia into individual parfait cups or small dishes. Cover and cool in the fridge for at least 1 hour to set and chill. Before serving, add a generous dollop of whipped topping or whipped cream and a maraschino cherry on top.

this would be just darling served in little mason jars too! xo

taco SALAD

this taco salad—served in my mama's big yellow Tupperware bowl—is one of the most vivid memories of my childhood. It was always on the potluck table after church, and there was never any left over because everyone knows that salads with chips in them are the best salads.

Makes 8 to 12 servings

INGREDIENTS

1 pound ground beef, cooked
Garlic salt
Black pepper
2 heads iceberg lettuce, chopped
1 cup shredded Cheddar cheese
½ red onion, diced
2 medium vine-ripe tomatoes, diced
1 (15-ounce) can pinto beans, drained and rinsed
2 avocados, diced
1 cup buttermilk ranch dressing
4 handfuls Doritos, crumbled

PREPARATION

1. In a skillet cook the ground beef over medium-high heat, seasoning with garlic salt and pepper to taste. Set aside and allow to cool.

2. If you're going to eat the salad right away, toss together all of the ingredients in a large bowl.

3. If not, leave out the avocados, dressing, and chips. Add those ingredients to the rest right before you eat so the salad will be as crunchy as possible.

take this to the potluck in tupperware for easy transport and then transfer to a prettier bowl to serve it. xo

abuelita sanchez was a family friend who gave this recipe to my daddy on the condition that he would follow her recipe directions exactly. It's got black and pinto beans, peppers, and bacon, and the flavors are out of this world. I've served these on the side of a burger and as the inside of a burrito, and no matter how you eat them, they're always delicious.

Makes 8 to 12 servings

INGREDIENTS

1 tablespoon vegetable or canola oil
1 medium onion, diced
1 pound bacon, cut up in approximately 1-inch squares (avoid peppered bacon)
6 garlic cloves, chopped
1 (4-ounce) can diced green chiles
1 teaspoon cumin
1 bunch cilantro, chopped
3 (15-ounce) cans pinto beans
1 (15-ounce) can black beans
Pinch of salt and black pepper

PREPARATION

1. Place a large skillet over medium-high heat with the oil. Once hot, add the onion and bacon, and cook until it begins to brown, about 5 to 8 minutes. Make sure to stir often.

2. Stir in the garlic, green chilies, and cumin. Cook for 1 to 2 minutes to develop the flavor. Stir in the cilantro right at the end of the 2 minutes of sautéing, just to ensure that it holds its color and flavor.

3. Add the beans, including their liquid, and bring to a boil. Reduce heat to low, and simmer for about 5 minutes. Give the beans a taste and adjust seasoning as needed, adding a pinch of salt and black pepper to taste. Serve immediately. Leftovers can be stored in the fridge for up to 4 days.

like it really spicy? add in some diced jalapeño! xo

charro
BEANS

SEVEN-
layer
salad

this is a dish that you may give the side eye . . . until you taste it. There is no earthly reason why layers of veggies topped with mayonnaise should work together, but it totally does. Give it a try—I promise you won't be disappointed.

Makes 4 to 6 servings

INGREDIENTS

2 cups shredded iceberg lettuce
1 green bell pepper, chopped
1 red bell pepper, chopped
1 red onion, chopped
4 celery stalks, chopped
1 cup shredded Cheddar cheese
1½ cups frozen peas, thawed
1 cup mayonnaise

PREPARATION

Layer each ingredient in a tall, round vase or trifle dish. Start with the lettuce and then go down the ingredient list, ending with the mayonnaise. Cover tightly with plastic wrap and store in the fridge until ready to eat.

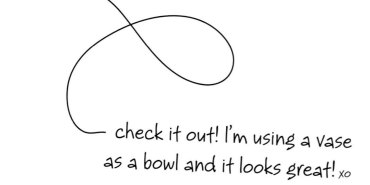

check it out! I'm using a vase as a bowl and it looks great! xo

guys, just think of these as really fancy baked potatoes. The hardest part is slicing the potatoes (which isn't hard at all), and they're awesome because you can "stuff" them with just about anything. My favorites? Bacon and Cheddar or some of my barbecue root beer chicken with red onion.

Makes 12 potatoes

INGREDIENTS

12 medium-size Yukon gold potatoes, rinsed and dried
¼ cup extra-virgin olive oil
3 tablespoons fresh parsley, chopped
3 tablespoons fresh thyme, chopped
3 tablespoons fresh chives, chopped
3 tablespoons fresh rosemary, chopped
4 garlic cloves, minced
1 teaspoon salt
1 teaspoon black pepper
½ cup grated Parmesan

PREPARATION

1. Preheat the oven to 450°F. Line a baking sheet with parchment paper and set aside.

2. Thinly slice the potatoes into rounds, but don't cut all the way through the potato. You want to create an accordion but still want the slices to stay together. Arrange the sliced potatoes on the prepared baking sheet.

3. Drizzle the potatoes with olive oil, making sure the oil falls in between the slices. In a small bowl, combine the herbs, garlic, salt, and pepper.

4. Sprinkle each potato liberally with the mixture, again making sure the mixture falls in between the slices of each potato.

5. Bake for 40 to 45 minutes until potatoes are crispy and golden brown. Midway through baking, baste the potatoes with the olive oil on the baking sheet. Remove from the oven and sprinkle with Parmesan. Serve immediately.

GARLIC *and* HERB
accordion
potatoes

fruit SALAD *with* raspberry dressing

because so many people

know how to make a fruit salad, it's easy for this to be a dish you don't put much thought or energy into. But if you add a homemade raspberry dressing you can turn a collection of fruit into a masterpiece.

Makes 8 to 12 servings

INGREDIENTS

For the dressing:
½ cup fresh raspberries
3 tablespoons red wine vinegar
¼ cup plus 1 tablespoon granulated sugar
Pinch of salt
½ teaspoon Dijon mustard
½ cup canola oil
½ teaspoon poppy seeds

1 pint strawberries, hulled and cut in half
1 cup blueberries
1 cup raspberries
1 cup blackberries
2 cups grapes
1 (8-ounce) can diced pineapple, drained
4 kiwifruit, sliced
2 green apples, cored and diced
2 red apples, cored and diced
½ cantaloupe, diced
½ honeydew, diced
1 mango, peeled and sliced

PREPARATION

1. To make the dressing, muddle berries in a Mason jar. Next, combine with all the other ingredients and add a tight-fitting lid. Shake vigorously until well combined.

2. In a large bowl, toss all of the fruit with enough dressing to coat everything. Serve immediately.

seasonal fruit is always best, so use a mixture of whatever is fresh. xo

spaghetti *salad*

this is another one of my mom's classic dishes. We didn't always have macaroni or fusilli for the pasta salad, so she started making "spaghetti salad." It's one of those things you'll be all judgy about until you give it a try, and then you'll understand why this is a staple for every family summer cookout.

Makes 4 to 6 servings

INGREDIENTS

1-pound package spaghetti noodles
1½ cups zesty Italian dressing
2 tablespoons McCormick's Salad Supreme seasoning
1 green bell pepper, chopped
1 (2.5-ounce) can sliced black olives
2 medium carrots, peeled and shredded
1 cup cherry tomatoes

PREPARATION

1. Bring a large pot of cold water to a boil and season liberally with salt. Boil spaghetti noodles according to package's directions until al dente, drain, and rinse with cold water (otherwise they will continue to cook, and you don't want them mushy).

2. In a large bowl, toss the noodles with the Italian dressing immediately. If you wait to do this the noodles will stick together.

3. Add the seasoning and veggies and toss to evenly combine. Store in the fridge and serve cold.

I've used other vegetables for this dish, including broccoli, artichoke, red onion, and cucumber. xo

leftovers

I would just like to state for the record that I think having a leftover chapter is the greatest idea I've ever come up with in my adult life. I know what you're thinking, *the best idea you've ever come up with is how to use leftover meat loaf?* Yep! This section is a collection of new recipes you can make using the leftovers from other recipes in this book. This idea comes from growing up as the child of a woman who could look into a fridge holding mustard and three eggs and somehow use that to create Thanksgiving dinner for fourteen people. Where I come from, that's called working with what you've got. A newer vernacular might call it sustainability. Either way, I call it good eats!

LEFTOVERS

FRIED *burritos*
(from tamale pie, page 75)

the fried burrito was one of my mom's specialties because she had clued into one of the great truths in life. If you cover it in cheese and fry it in a tortilla, kids will eat almost anything. She did this with everything from leftover spaghetti sauce with mozzarella to cherry pie filling and cream cheese sprinkled with cinnamon and sugar. Obviously not a healthy choice for every day, but as a weekend treat, it's a great way to use up leftovers.

//

Makes 4 to 6 burritos

INGREDIENTS

2 cups vegetable oil, for frying
6 medium flour tortillas or 4 large
2 cups leftover Tamale Pie (page 75)
1 cup shredded Cheddar cheese
Sour cream, for topping
Salsa, for topping
Scallions, for topping
Sliced black olives, for topping

PREPARATION

1. In a large skillet, fill halfway with oil and heat over medium-high heat.

2. In smaller dry skillet, warm the flour tortillas over medium-high heat to make them pliable. Off heat, fill each tortilla with a few spoonfuls of tamale pie. Sprinkle with cheese and roll the filled tortilla into a tight burrito.

3. Carefully place the burrito into the oil, seam side down. Fry the burritos, about two at a time, until golden brown and crispy on both sides. Transfer the burritos to a plate lined with paper towels to soak up excess grease. Serve topped with sour cream, salsa, scallions, and black olives.

these are awesome for game day! xo

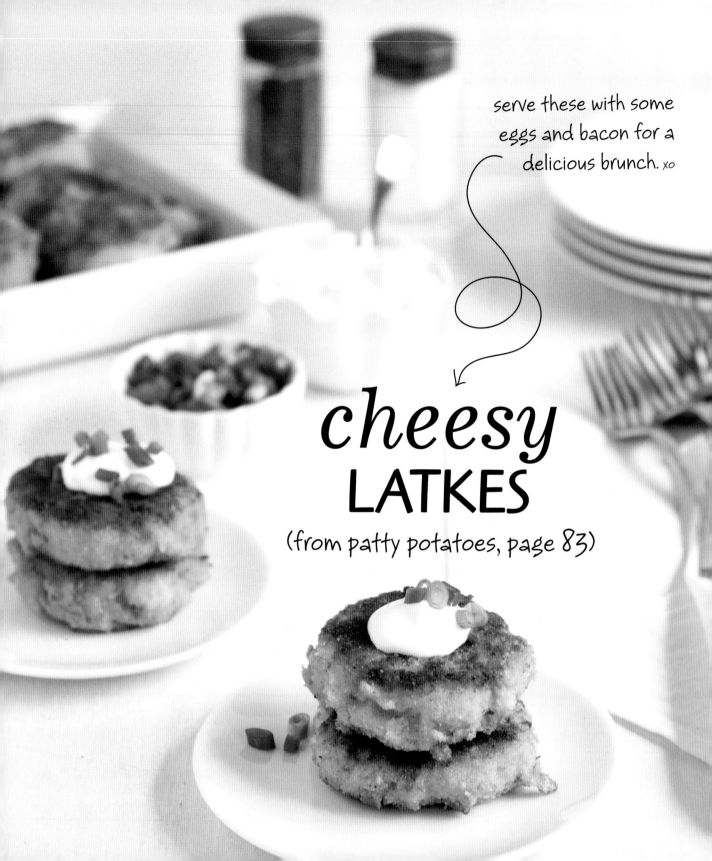

serve these with some eggs and bacon for a delicious brunch. xo

cheesy
LATKES

(from patty potatoes, page 83)

remember how i told you that my mother-in-law always makes Patty Potatoes? Well, one year at Christmas, some were miraculously left over, and my father-in-law (in a genius maneuver we still talk about to this day) got up the next morning and fried them in little patties to go along with our breakfast. It's cheese potatoes fried into a potato pancake, and holy Moses, it's so good!

Makes about 16

INGREDIENTS

1 cup shredded cheese—try Cheddar,
mozzarella, or Pepper Jack for some heat
2 cups leftover Patty Potatoes (page 83), chilled
3 large eggs
2 tablespoons milk
1 teaspoon salt
½ teaspoon black pepper
1½ cups plain bread crumbs
4 tablespoons olive oil, for frying
Sour cream, for topping
Sliced scallions, for garnish

PREPARATION

1. In a medium bowl, mix the shredded cheese with the Patty Potatoes.

2. Shape into small patties and place them on a plate.

3. In a large bowl, whisk the eggs, milk, salt, and pepper. Place the bread crumbs in a shallow bowl. Dredge the potato patties in the egg mixture and then in the bread crumbs to fully coat.

4. In a large skillet, heat olive oil over medium-high heat. Once hot, fry the patties, a few at a time, until golden brown and crispy on both sides.

5. Serve with a dollop of sour cream and a sprinkling of scallions.

if you have leftover carnitas, this is a great way to use them with a totally different flavor palate. Consider it for a weekend lunch or a summer dinner paired with the slow cooker baked beans.

Makes 4 sandwiches

INGREDIENTS

2 cups leftover Mango Chipotle Carnitas (page 101)
2 cups shredded coleslaw mix
¾ cup mayonnaise
1 teaspoon celery salt
1 tablespoon apple cider vinegar
4 hamburger buns or rolls
1 large avocado, sliced
2 tomatoes, sliced

PREPARATION

1. In a large bowl, mix the coleslaw mix, mayonnaise, celery salt, and vinegar. Cover and chill for at least 30 minutes.

2. Rewarm the carnitas in the microwave for about 2 to 5 minutes or in a saucepan over low heat for about 8 to 10 minutes.

3. To assemble the sandwiches, toast the buns and fill with the warm carnitas. Top with coleslaw, avocado slices, and tomato.

this sandwich would be perfect with the beer limeade on page 203. xo

spicy
pulled PORK
sandwiches
(from carnitas, page 101)

breakfast
SCRAMBLE
(from accordion potatoes, page 134)

make the accordion potatoes as a side dish for your dinner and then you can use the extra to make a breakfast scramble the next morning. You're a kitchen all-star!

Makes 4 to 6 servings

INGREDIENTS

2 tablespoons salted butter
½ cup diced ham
½ medium red bell pepper, sliced
½ medium yellow bell pepper, sliced
½ red onion, sliced
1 cup button mushrooms, sliced
3 to 4 Accordion Potatoes (page 134), chopped
6 large eggs
2 tablespoons milk
1 teaspoon salt
½ teaspoon black pepper
½ cup shredded cheese—try Cheddar,
mozzarella, or Pepper Jack for some heat

PREPARATION

1. In a large skillet, melt the butter over medium-high heat. Add the ham, veggies, and potatoes, and cook until browned, 5 to 8 minutes.

2. In a large bowl, whisk the eggs, milk, salt, and black pepper. Pour the eggs into the skillet with the veggies and cook, stirring often, until the eggs are no longer runny.

3. Fold in the cheese and serve with warm toast on the side.

CHEESY
crispy **wontons**

(from any dip)

any dip, you guys! Think of it . . . you can take any of the leftover dip and put it inside this little deep-fried pocket. It's basically like having chips and dipping sauce in one handy compartment.

//

Makes about 2 dozen

INGREDIENTS

2 cups vegetable oil, for frying
24 wonton wrappers
1½ cups leftover Spinach Artichoke Dip (page 61)
1 cup balsamic dressing, for dipping

PREPARATION

1. In a large skillet, fill halfway with oil and heat over medium-high heat.

2. Fill each wonton wrapper with 1 to 2 teaspoons of dip.

3. Fold the wrapper to make a pocket and seal the edges with a bit of water.

4. Carefully fry the wontons, a few at a time, until golden brown and crispy on both sides. Transfer to a plate lined with paper towel to soak up excess oil. Serve with balsamic dressing on the side for dipping.

my favorite dip to serve inside crispy little pockets of wonton? spinach artichoke, obviously! xo

pot roast has such a great

flavor that it begs to be used as a filling. Here, I just chop it up, veggies and all, add some cheese, and tuck it inside some frozen pie dough. I love to eat these pies hot out of the oven, but they're good at room temperature, too, so it would make a great addition to your picnic basket or tailgate party.

Makes about 10 hand pies

INGREDIENTS

1 package refrigerated pie dough (double crust)
1 cup leftover Balsamic Pot Roast (page 113)
1 cup shredded Cheddar cheese
1 large egg, whisked with a splash of water
Fresh thyme, for garnish

PREPARATION

1. Preheat the oven to 375°F. Line two baking sheets with parchment paper and set aside.

2. Unroll the dough and use a cookie cutter to cut out circles for mini pies, and set aside.

3. Cut your pot roast into smaller pieces. In a large bowl, mix the pot roast with the cheese. Place a spoonful of the pot roast mixture into the center of each dough circle. Fold the dough over to create a half circle and seal the edges with a bit of water, then crimp them with a fork. Transfer to the prepared baking sheets.

4. Brush the pies with egg wash and bake for 15 to 20 minutes or until golden brown. Garnish with thyme and serve.

this is a fun dish to prep with
your kiddos, my boys love them! xo

pot roast
HAND pies
(from balsamic pot roast, page 113)

BBQ *chicken*
quesadillas

(from bbq root beer
chicken, page 110)

how often do you consider making a hearty quesadilla for a weeknight dinner? My guess is, not often enough. It's a great option to use up leftover shredded meat, and it's super kid friendly. Think about it—between the cheese, meat, bread, and veggies these have the same elements as a pizza delivery, only this doesn't cost any extra money and can be cooked in a few minutes.

Makes 6 quesadillas

INGREDIENTS

12 large flour tortillas
½ cup barbecue sauce
3 cups shredded Cheddar and Jack cheese blend
2 cups leftover Root Beer Chicken (page 110), shredded
½ red onion, diced
5 scallions, sliced (about ½ cup)

PREPARATION

1. In a dry skillet, heat the tortillas over medium-high heat to make them pliable. Keep the skillet over medium-high heat.

2. Spread a few tablespoons of barbecue sauce on each tortilla.

3. Sprinkle with cheese, shredded chicken, red onion, and scallions. Top with another tortilla and press down. In the dry skillet, cook the quesadilla, turning once, until it's crispy and the cheese has melted. Cut the quesadillas into wedges and serve.

leave off the onions if your kids don't like them; it'll still be delicious! xo

FRUIT salad *smoothie*

(from fruit salad, page 137)

maybe it's because I make too much of it, maybe it's because people don't want to fill their plate with a healthy option when there are so many yummy starches on the party buffet, but either way I always have leftover fruit salad. This is a great way to make sure all of that delicious fruit doesn't go to waste. Also, you can freeze some of it for smoothies later in the week.

Makes 6 smoothies

INGREDIENTS

3 cups leftover Fruit Salad (page 137)
1 cup plain or vanilla Greek yogurt
2 cups ice
½ cup soy or almond milk
3 tablespoons leftover Raspberry Dressing (page 137)

PREPARATION

Combine all of the ingredients in a blender and blend on high until smooth.

I add whey protein powder and chia seeds to make this a great healthy breakfast. xo

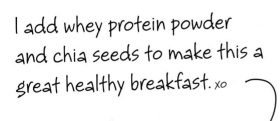

mmm, meat loaf sliders.

Just typing the name out makes me hungry. It's like a normal slider only a hundred times more delicious. Sure, you could just make regular-size burgers, but where's the fun in that? Plus, if you make them small then you can eat twice as many.

Makes 12 sliders

INGREDIENTS

16 slices leftover Balsamic Meat Loaf (page 76), cut in half
12 dinner rolls (I love Hawaiian rolls for this)
¼ cup ketchup (mayonnaise or mustard works, too)
6 slices mozzarella cheese, cut in half
2 cups baby spinach
1 cup crispy fried onions

PREPARATION

1. Cut leftover meat loaf into squares small enough to fit on your rolls. Place on a plate and zap in the microwave until warmed through, about 2 to 3 minutes.

2. Split the dinner rolls in half and spread with ketchup or a mixture of mayo and mustard . . . or all three!

3. Top bread with a piece of meat loaf, mozzarella cheese, baby spinach, and crispy onions. Serve warm or at room temperature.

these make a yummy appetizer or delicious lunch. xo

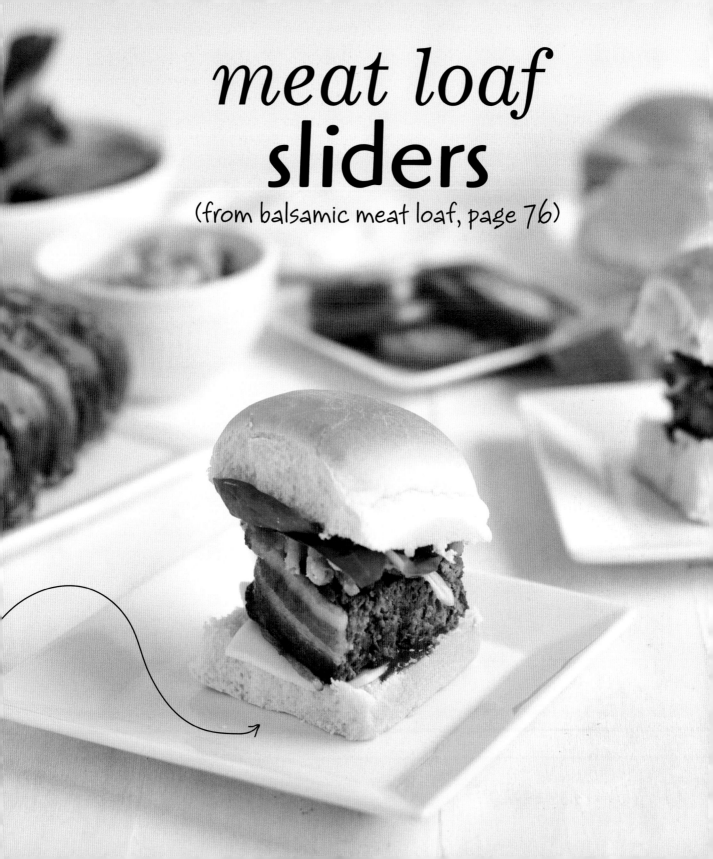

meat loaf
sliders
(from balsamic meat loaf, page 76)

TUNA
noodle
croquettes

(from aunt linda's tuna casserole, page 88)

i often have leftovers of casseroles, and I like to get inventive with ways to adjust the flavor in the original dish. These croquettes make a great appetizer, but I've also eaten them for dinner.

Makes 12 to 15 croquettes

INGREDIENTS

1½ cups leftover Aunt Linda's Tuna Casserole (page 88)
2 teaspoons Dijon mustard
2 large egg yolks, beaten
2 tablespoons all-purpose flour
1 large egg, beaten
2 cups plain bread crumbs
2 cups vegetable oil, for frying

PREPARATION

1. In a large bowl, mix the tuna casserole with the Dijon mustard, egg yolks, and flour until evenly incorporated. Form into small ovals and place on a plate or platter.

2. Place the beaten egg in shallow bowl and the bread crumbs in a separate shallow bowl. Dredge croquettes in the egg and then in the bread crumbs.

3. In a large skillet, fill halfway with vegetable oil and heat over medium-high heat. Once the oil is hot, drop in the croquettes, a few at a time, and fry until golden brown and crispy on both sides, 2 to 3 minutes. Transfer to a plate lined with paper towels. Place on paper towels to soak up excess oil and serve warm.

this dress was in the closet of our house when we moved in... all it took was a little tailoring to make it adorable

watch the clearance racks after christmas, that's when I find the most darling cake stands

somethin' sweet

Although I do believe in moderation, I don't believe in skipping dessert. There are too many incredible treats out there to even contemplate passing them up. Mile-high mud pie, vanilla ice cream with a scoop of peanut butter, those Costco cakes with the cream cheese filling, whole sleeves of Girl Scout cookies—why on earth would you want to miss out? I think a great meal just begs for a bite of somethin' sweet to finish it off. It was hard to choose only ten options for this section, but rest assured, these are ten of my best. These cookies, puddings, pies, and cakes have been doctored, decorated, and passed down from one generation to the next. Enjoy them with your afternoon cup of coffee or as your midnight snack, so long as you enjoy them. Life is too short not to have some sugar once in a while.

SOMETHIN' SWEET

mema's CARROT *cake*

my mema has all sorts of great recipes. Her German chocolate cake is incredible. Her fried potatoes will make you cry, they're so good. But her best-in-show is without a doubt her carrot cake. Moist and delicious and topped with a cream cheese icing, each slice will make you gain, like, twelve pounds at least, but you won't even care.

Makes 8 to 12 servings
INGREDIENTS

For the cake:
4 large eggs
1½ cups vegetable or canola oil
2 cups sugar
2 cups shredded carrots
1 (8-ounce) can crushed pineapple
1 teaspoon vanilla
2 cups all-purpose flour
1½ teaspoons baking soda
Dash of salt
2 teaspoons cinnamon

For the frosting:
1 (8-ounce) package cream cheese, room temperature
¼ pound (1 stick) salted butter, room temperature
3 cups powdered sugar
1 teaspoon vanilla

PREPARATION

1. Preheat the oven to 350°F. Grease and flour three 8-inch round cake pans and set aside.

2. In a large mixing bowl, mix the eggs, oil, sugar, carrots, pineapple, and vanilla. In a separate bowl, sift the remaining dry ingredients together. Gradually mix the dry ingredients in with the wet ingredients until well blended.

3. Pour the batter into the prepared cake pans, filling about ¾ of the way. Bake for 40 to 45 minutes or until a toothpick inserted in the center comes out clean. The tops should be a golden brown. Allow to cool completely.

4. While the cakes cool, in a large mixing bowl, beat all the frosting ingredients until light and fluffy.

5. Frost the cakes in between each layer and top (leaving the sides bare). Cut and serve.

jell-o PRETZEL *salad*

i'll be honest. The first time someone showed up to our house with a Jell-O Pretzel Salad I was like, *what the what, what?* There's a salad with pretzels and Jell-O inside? The first thing I discovered is that there isn't anything salad-like about this dish. The second thing I discovered is that it's delicious! There are a million variations online and you can use any Jell-O recipe your heart desires. This one is berry flavored, so the red, white, and blue make it the perfect dessert for the Fourth of July.

Makes 6 servings

INGREDIENTS

2 cups crushed pretzels
4 tablespoons (½ stick) unsalted butter, melted
3 tablespoons granulated sugar
1 (8-ounce) package cream cheese, softened
1 (8-ounce) container frozen whipped topping
¾ cup powdered sugar
1 (6-ounce) box blueberry Jell-O
1 pint each fresh blueberries, raspberries, and blackberries
1 (8-ounce) can crushed pineapple

PREPARATION

1. Preheat the oven to 375°F.

2. In a large bowl, mix the crushed pretzels, melted butter, and granulated sugar. Evenly spread the mixture on a baking sheet. Bake for about 10 minutes or until golden brown. Allow to cool.

3. Divide the pretzels mixture among 6 mini trifle dishes and flatten in an even layer.

4. In a medium bowl, beat the cream cheese, whipped topping, and powdered sugar until completely smooth. Divide among the mini trifle dishes (on top of the pretzel layer) and spread with the back of a spoon.

5. In a medium bowl, dissolve the Jell-O in 2 cups of boiling water. Allow to slightly cool. Stir in the fresh berries and crushed pineapple. Divide among the mini trifle dishes (on top of the cream layer) and spread evenly. Allow to chill in the fridge, covered with plastic wrap, until set, about 3 hours. Garnish with a dollop of whipped topping. Enjoy!

i don't know when my mother started adding orange zest to her sugar cookies. I only know that this flavor has always been a part of some of my favorite memories of baking with her. This recipe works great with any cookie cutter, with icing, or as a sweet unfrosted treat with your afternoon coffee.

Makes 3 dozen cookies

INGREDIENTS

2 large eggs
1 tablespoon vanilla extract
8 teaspoons milk
Zest from 2 medium oranges
1½ cups sugar
1⅓ cups butter-flavored Crisco
4 cups all-purpose flour
3 teaspoons baking powder

PREPARATION

1. Preheat the oven to 350°F. Line two baking sheets with parchment paper and set aside.

2. In a large mixing bowl, mix the eggs, vanilla, milk, zest, sugar, and Crisco until well combined.

3. Slowly mix in the flour and baking powder until completely combined.

4. Roll out the cookie dough on a floured surface (or between two pieces of wax paper) until the dough is about ½ inch thick. Dip a cookie cutter into flour to prevent sticking and cut out the cookies. Place on the prepared baking sheets and bake for about 10 minutes or until lightly golden brown around the edges. Allow the cookies to cool on a wire rack before eating.

these freeze really well and defrost quickly, so make an extra batch and keep in the freezer for unexpected guests. xo

ORANGE *sugar* cookies

MISSOURI
cookies

i have no earthly idea why we called these "Missouri Cookies" in our house. I'm not even sure if that's what everyone calls them or if in other places they're "Milwaukee Cookies" or "Mississippi Cookies." I do know that they're a no-bake recipe. Being a no-bake recipe makes them great for summer when you want a treat but don't want to heat up the house with the oven.

Makes 2 dozen cookies

INGREDIENTS

2 cups sugar
3 tablespoons cocoa powder
¼ pound (1 stick) margarine
½ cup milk
½ cup peanut butter
1 teaspoon vanilla extract
3 cups old-fashioned rolled oats
Pinch of salt

PREPARATION

1. Line two baking sheets with parchment paper and set aside.

2. In a large pot, mix the sugar, cocoa, margarine, and milk over medium-high heat. Stir until the margarine is melted. Cook, stirring, until the mixture comes to a boil, about 5 minutes.

3. Remove from the heat and stir in the remaining ingredients until well combined.

4. Using a medium ice-cream scoop or two spoons, portion out the cookie dough into even mounds onto the prepared baking sheets.

5. Allow to cool down to room temperature or in the fridge until set.

tie the spoon to the glass
with a ribbon for a cute
presentation for a party. xo

BANANA
pudding
parfaits

making banana pudding was always my job as a little girl. It was one of the first things I was ever allowed to "cook" by myself. I'd set up at the counter with a butter knife to cut the bananas, then I'd make the pudding and layer it all into a big glass bowl. As an adult it's still one of my favorites, but I like to serve it in tall shot glasses with a demitasse spoon. The unique presentation gives new life to a classic recipe.

Makes 6 to 8 servings

INGREDIENTS

1 (1-ounce) box instant vanilla pudding mix
2 cups milk
2 cups heavy whipping cream
3 tablespoons powdered sugar
1 teaspoon vanilla extract
2 cups mini vanilla wafer cookies
3 ripe bananas, sliced

PREPARATION

1. In a large bowl, whisk the pudding mix and milk until smooth and evenly combined. Cover with plastic wrap and place in the fridge until chilled.

2. Beat the whipping cream with an electric mixer on high until somewhat thick. Mix in the sugar and vanilla extract and continue to whip until soft peaks form.

3. Transfer the pudding into a large plastic food storage bag and the whipped cream in a separate bag. Snip off a corner on both and use them as piping bags.

4. Layer the pudding, cream, wafer cookies, and sliced bananas in mini parfait glasses, alternating between each to create multiple layers in each glass. Cover with plastic wrap and place in the fridge to chill until ready to serve.

you could always count on two things in my grandma Neeley's kitchen: apple cake on the table and sweet tea on the stove. Her old aluminum cake pan was forever filled with this moist, flavorful dessert that my siblings and I ate by the truckload. Grandma has long since gone to heaven, but when I start missing her I bake this recipe and remember all those summers I spent in her kitchen.

Makes 9 servings

INGREDIENTS

¼ cup shortening
1 cup sugar
2 large eggs
1 cup flour
1 teaspoon baking powder
2 teaspoons cinnamon
¼ teaspoon salt
¼ teaspoon nutmeg
1 to 2 medium apples, peeled and chopped (about 2 cups)

PREPARATION

1. Preheat the oven to 350°F. Grease an 8-inch square cake pan and set aside.

2. In a large bowl, cream the shortening and sugar. In a separate bowl, whisk the eggs, then add the eggs to the shortening mixture and stir to combine.

3. In a separate bowl, mix all the dry ingredients except the apples, then combine with the wet ingredients. Fold in the apples.

4. Pour the batter into the prepared cake pan and bake for 35 minutes or until a cake tester inserted in the center comes out clean. This cake is great with coffee for a brunch or add vanilla ice cream for a tasty dessert.

this is delicious plain and absolute heaven when you add a scoop of ice cream! xo

grandma neeley's
apple
CAKE

NO-BAKE *cheesecakes* in a *jar*

i feel like at this point you've probably caught on to my love of Mason jars. Seriously, why does putting something inside of one make it instantly a thousand times cuter? No-bake cheesecake? I guess. No-bake cheesecakes in a Mason jar with a berry garnish? Your dessert game just got bumped up to a whole new level!

Makes 6 individual cheesecakes

INGREDIENTS

For the crust:
1½ cups graham cracker crumbs (6 to 8 full graham crackers)
2 tablespoons granulated sugar
½ teaspoon salt
6 tablespoons unsalted butter, melted

For the filling:
1 (8-ounce) package cream cheese, softened
½ cup sweetened condensed milk
1 tablespoon fresh lemon juice
1 teaspoon vanilla extract
½ pint fresh blueberries, rinsed
½ pint fresh raspberries, rinsed
½ pint fresh blackberries, rinsed
1 cup sliced fresh strawberries
Fresh mint, for garnish

PREPARATION

1. In a medium bowl, combine the graham cracker crumbs, sugar, salt, and melted butter. Mix until evenly moistened.

2. Divide the crust among 6 small jars. Press down the crumbs with a spoon or your fingers. Place the jars in the freezer for about 10 minutes to firm up.

3. In a seperate bowl, cream together the cream cheese, sweetened condensed milk, lemon juice, and vanilla extract until fluffy and smooth. Transfer to a piping bag or large food storage bag with the end snipped off. Pipe out a thin layer of cheesecake filling on top of the crust. Sprinkle with fresh berries and top with another layer of cheesecake filling.

4. Finish off with a few more berries and a mint leaf. Cover with plastic wrap and chill in the fridge for at least 30 minutes before serving. Enjoy!

if you came to our house for dinner when I was growing up, you'd get Texas Sheet Cake for dessert. In fact, if I ever came in the house from playing and smelled cinnamon and chocolate baking in the oven I knew we'd be having guests for dinner. Serve the cake up with a scoop of vanilla ice cream, or if you're really feeling it add some whipped cream and chopped almonds for good measure.

Makes 10 to 12 servings

INGREDIENTS

For the cake:
½ pound (2 sticks) unsalted butter
¼ cup unsweetened cocoa powder
1 cup water
2 cups all-purpose flour
1½ cups firmly packed light-brown sugar
1 teaspoon baking soda
1½ teaspoons cinnamon
½ teaspoon salt
⅓ cup from (14-ounce) can sweetened condensed milk (reserve remaining for glaze)
2 eggs

For the glaze:
¼ pound (1 stick) unsalted butter
½ cup unsweetened cocoa powder
Remaining condensed milk
2 cups powdered sugar
2 cups chopped nuts (peanuts or pecans)
Ice cream for serving

PREPARATION

1. Preheat the oven to 350°F. Grease a 15 by 10-inch jelly roll baking sheet with butter and set aside.

2. In a medium pot, melt together ½ pound butter, ¼ cup cocoa powder, and 1 cup of water over medium-high heat. Cook until the mixture comes to a boil. Remove the pot from the heat, allowing the mixture to cool down slightly.

3. In a large mixing bowl, combine the flour, brown sugar, baking soda, cinnamon, and salt.

4. In a separate bowl, whisk ⅓ cup condensed milk, eggs, and the melted chocolate butter mixture. Pour into the dry ingredients and stir until evenly combined.

5. Pour the cake batter into the prepared baking sheet. Bake for about 15 minutes or until a toothpick inserted in the middle comes out clean.

6. In the meantime, make the glaze. In a small pot, combine butter, cocoa, and the remaining condensed milk. Cook until it simmers. Remove from the heat and stir in the powdered sugar and chopped nuts.

7. Pour the glaze over the baked cake and spread evenly over the top. Allow the glaze to set before cutting. Serve with a scoop of ice cream.

texas sheet CAKE

raspberry *peach* DUMP *cake*

a dump cake is exactly what it sounds like. Go into your pantry, gather a bunch of ingredients, dump it all into a pan, bake it in the oven, and voilà! You have a delicious dump cake. I love that you can change this recipe depending on what you have on hand and it will always be delicious. My absolute favorite is raspberry peach because the combination is as pretty as it is tasty.

Makes 8 to 12 servings

INGREDIENTS

1 (29-ounce) can peaches (in syrup)
1 pint fresh or frozen raspberries (thawed if frozen)
1 box white cake mix
¼ pound plus 4 tablespoons (1½ sticks) unsalted butter
Frozen whipped topping, for serving

PREPARATION

1. Preheat the oven to 350°F. Lightly grease a Bundt pan, tube pan, or a 9 by 13-inch baking dish with cooking spray.

2. Dump the peaches (with their syrup) into your baking pan. Sprinkle with the raspberries. Top with the cake mix in an even layer. Slice the butter and distribute in an even layer on top of the cake mix.

3. Bake until the top is golden brown and bubbly, 45 minutes to 1 hour. Serve with a dollop of whipped topping.

change up the boxed cake mix to chocolate or strawberry for a fun flavor swap. xo

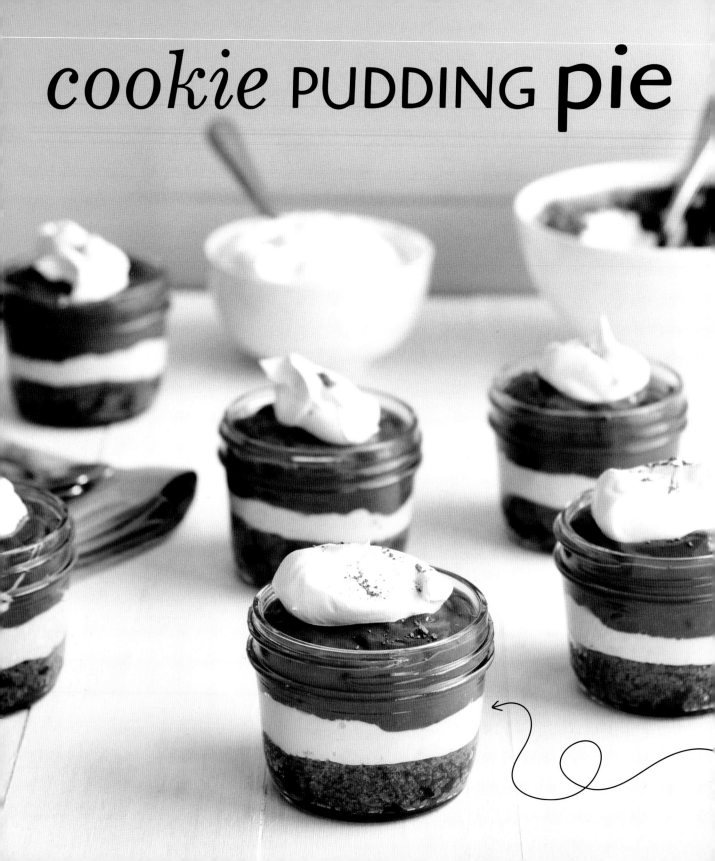

cookie PUDDING pie

how to best describe the miracle that is cookie pudding pie? Imagine a giant chocolate-chip cookie crust topped with chocolate pudding, then you add powdered sugar and cream cheese mixed together. *Then* you top that with whipped cream. I mean, seriously? In terms of miracles, it's right up there with the Lord walking on water.

Makes 6 servings

INGREDIENTS

1 (16.5-ounce) package refrigerated chocolate-chip cookie dough
(I recommend the tube because it's easy to squeeze into the ramekins)
1 (3.9-ounce) package Jell-O instant chocolate pudding
2 cups whole milk
1 (8-ounce) package cream cheese, softened
2 cups powdered sugar
1 (8-ounce) container frozen whipped topping

PREPARATION

1. Preheat the oven to 350°F. Grease 6 ramekins with cooking spray. Divide the cookie dough among the ramekins and press down into an even layer. Bake according to the package instructions, slightly undercooking them a few minutes. Remove from the oven and allow to cool.

2. Make the chocolate pudding per package instructions with the milk, and put in the fridge to chill.

3. While the cookie crusts cool, in a large bowl, use an electric mixer to whip the cream cheese and powdered sugar.

4. Using a butter knife or spoon, add a layer of the cream cheese filling to the top of your cooled cookie crust. On top of the cream cheese add a generous layer of your chocolate pudding. Top the chocolate pudding with the frozen whipped topping and place in the fridge to chill until ready to serve.

you usually find this served in one big dish, but I like to serve it in mason jars as individual desserts. xo

sips

I fully admit to being a lover of anything involving alcohol. That includes wine, beer, and, most especially, beautifully crafted cocktails. My first experience with cocktails was when my big sister Chrissy let me have some of her Midori sour way before I was of legal drinking age—don't tell my mom—and I've loved cocktails ever since. Even if you don't drink alcohol, a good hostess always has something for her guests to sip on. Whether you like an ice-cold glass of sweet tea or some church punch with raspberry sherbet, this section includes great options for everybody.

SIPS

grandma's **SWEET** *tea*

my grandma opal always had a pitcher of sweet tea in her kitchen, and she always made it exactly the same way. There's nothing particularly special about it, except for maybe the shocking amount of sugar she added to get it to taste just right. Nowadays I only make it on special occasions, but I still use her same glass pitcher and boil it up just the way she did.

Makes 6 to 8 servings

INGREDIENTS

8 cups water
5 black tea bags
1 cup sugar
Ice
Fresh lemon slices, for garnish

PREPARATION

1. Fill a pot or a kettle with 8 cups of water, add the tea bags, and bring to a boil.

2. Pour in the sugar (yes, I know that's an ungodly amount of sweetener but that's the way it's done!) while the tea is still hot.

3. If you're serving this to company you can put the tea into a nice pitcher. However you present it, make sure you serve it over a lot of ice and a lemon slice to garnish.

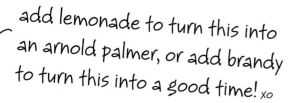

add lemonade to turn this into an arnold palmer, or add brandy to turn this into a good time! xo

i had my first mint julep

a couple of years ago. Dave and I were in Louisiana and they offered us a drink. It was strong enough to take the varnish off an old car and so sweet it made my teeth hurt. I loved it. This version is so good that even NoLa residents will be like, *What is this magical cocktail?* And I'll be like, *That's my blackberry mint julep. Go Saints!*

Makes 4 cocktails

INGREDIENTS

½ cup water
½ cup granulated sugar
½ cup fresh blackberries, plus more for garnish
½ cup fresh mint leaves, loosely packed, plus more for garnish
4 ounces bourbon whiskey
Shaved ice

PREPARATION

1. In a small saucepan, combine ½ cup water and the granulated sugar and bring to a simmer over medium-high heat. Continue to cook for about 5 minutes, or until the sugar has dissolved. Set aside and cool completely.

2. Depending on how big your cocktail shaker is, you're probably going to have to do this in batches. Start by adding the blackberries and mint to the bottom of the shaker. Using a small spoon or wooden spoon, muddle the ingredients together to develop their natural flavor.

3. Throw in the bourbon, simple syrup (as much or as little as you'd like depending on how sweet you'd like the drink) into the cocktail shaker, and shake vigorously to combine and extract the most flavor.

4. Pack 4 glasses with shaved ice.

5. Strain the drink into the glasses that have been packed with shaved ice. Garnish with a sprig of mint and a fresh blackberry. Enjoy!

blackberry MINT julep

MOSCOW mule

a moscow mule is so refreshing and so darn easy to make. I love serving this as the signature cocktail at a summer party or just making a couple for Dave and me to enjoy on the back patio on a Friday night. I put mine in any old thing I can find, but some purists insist these should only be served in copper mugs. Keep your eye out and snag them when you find them on sale.

//

Makes 4 servings

INGREDIENTS

Ice
16 to 24 ounces ginger beer
8 ounces vodka
2 limes, cut in half
Fresh lime slices, for garnish
Cucumber slices, for garnish
Mint leaves, for garnish

PREPARATION

1. Fill 4 short glasses (Moscow Mules are normally served in copper mugs) with a lot of ice.

2. Divide the ginger beer and vodka between the glasses.

3. Squeeze half a lime in each glass and give it a gentle stir.

4. Garnish with lime and cucumber slices and mint.

these are a great party drink, make a big batch and store in a pitcher so guests can serve themselves! xo

orange
SHERBET
church
punch

i'm sure this recipe actually has a name, but since we drank it at every baby shower, bridal shower, and women's prayer meeting held in the fellowship hall at church, I always just called it Church Punch. You can make it with any flavor sherbet, but I'm a big fan of orange or the pretty pink of raspberry.

Makes 8 servings

INGREDIENTS

10 to 12 scoops orange sherbet
2 cans frozen orange juice concentrate (made according to can directions)
1 (64-ounce) bottle orange pineapple juice
1 (2-liter) bottle 7 Up or ginger ale
3 oranges, sliced
1 (8-ounce) can pineapple slices

PREPARATION

1. Scoop out the sherbet onto a baking sheet and freeze for several hours. You can do this the night before.

2. In a large punch bowl or pitcher, combine the orange juice made from the concentrate, orange pineapple juice, and soda. Throw in the orange and pineapple slices.

3. Right before serving, drop in the sherbet scoops. Serve immediately.

i love the fourth of july. It's
been one of my favorite holidays since I was
a little girl, and now that I have my own kids,
I want to make it as special as possible. This
punch is such a fun way to add to the red,
white, and blue festivities.

Makes 8 servings

INGREDIENTS

1½ cups fresh blueberries
1 cup fresh sliced strawberries
1 large jicama
2 cups white grape juice
2 cups apple juice
2 cups ginger ale

PREPARATION

1. To make the fruit ice cubes: Add the fresh blueberries and sliced
strawberries to an ice cube tray. Fill the tray with water and freeze
until firm. You can do this the night before.

2. Peel and cut the jicama into thin rounds. Cut out stars with a star-
shaped cookie cutter.

3. Mix the juices and ginger ale in a large pitcher and stir to
combine. Right before serving, add the fruit ice cubes and jicama
stars. Enjoy right away!

if you can't find jicama, cut your
stars out of honeydew melon. xo

patriotic
PUNCH

BEER
limeade

my big sister christina

suggested this recipe to me awhile ago and I remember thinking, *I've got to try that out!* Beer snobs might gag at the idea, but it's seriously really good. Chances are you're putting a lime in your Corona anyway, and this is just like that—only with a little sweetness to enhance the flavor.

Makes 6 to 8 servings

INGREDIENTS

1 can frozen limeade concentrate
¼ cup coarse salt
½ teaspoon cayenne pepper
Lime slices
Ice
6 Corona beers
2 tablespoons lime juice

PREPARATION

1. In a large pitcher make the limeade according to the can instructions. Place in the fridge to chill.

2. In a small, shallow dish, combine the salt and cayenne pepper.

3. Run a lime slice along the edge of each glass and then dunk each glass into the salt mixture, coating the rim all the way around.

4. Fill each glass with ice and pour in the limeade halfway up. Fill up each glass the rest of the way with beer and a bit of fresh lime juice in each. Garnish with a lime slice.

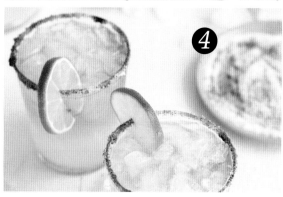

this is the perfect "side dish" for my grilled guacamole on page 67. xo

strawberry AND rosemary
moonshine

add a cute tag to turn
this shine into a hostess
gift or cool party favor! xo

it's moonshine, sort of. I mean, obviously, real moonshine is totally illegal, and I'd like to keep this cookbook on the right side of the law. But I did think it would be fun to make a version of our own since nothing screams down-home backwoods to me more than getting your shine on.

Makes 8 to 12 servings

INGREDIENTS

3 pints fresh strawberries, rinsed and sliced
4 limes, peeled and sliced
4 sprigs fresh rosemary
1 (1.75-liter) bottle vodka

PREPARATION

1. Divide the strawberries, lime slices, and rosemary sprigs among 4 large Mason jars.

2. Pour the vodka into each Mason jar, filling to the top of each.

3. Cover each tightly with a lid and store in the fridge. The longer the vodka is kept in the fridge, the stronger the flavors will be. These can be stored for up to 6 months.

4. When ready to use, strain out the strawberries, lime, and rosemary.

it turns out there are all kinds of names for this particular cocktail, but I always knew it as the Gypsy. It's red wine and Diet Coke. Believe me, I realize there is no earthly reason why this should work, but it does! The wine helps you relax, the caffeine helps you stay awake . . . this should be the signature cocktail for mothers everywhere!

Makes 4 servings

INGREDIENTS

Ice
1 bottle (750-ml) red wine (not too expensive)
2 cups (16 ounces) Diet Coke
1 cup fresh berries, for garnish

PREPARATION

1. Fill 4 tall glasses halfway with ice.

2. Divide the red wine evenly among the 4 glasses.

3. Top off each with Diet Coke, and garnish with fresh berries.

I used to drink this in my 20s, and years later I still think it's delicious! xo

gypsy

LEMON-LIME
margarita popsicles

don't get too frisky with
your liquor on this one.
too much tequila and the
pops won't freeze. xo

isn't this the cutest idea ever for a summer party cocktail? It's all the great flavors of a margarita you love, frozen on the end of a stick. For extra fun I add matching washi tape to the bottom of the Popsicle stick to make them even cuter.

Makes 8 servings

INGREDIENTS

¾ cup granulated sugar
¾ cup fresh lime juice
½ cup water
Juice from 1 orange
2 tablespoons fresh lemon juice
2 tablespoons tequila
2 tablespoons orange liqueur
Lime slices
Lemon slices
Popsicle sticks
Coarse salt

PREPARATION

1. In a small saucepan, combine the sugar, lime juice, water, orange juice, and lemon juice over medium heat. Cook, allowing the sugar to dissolve and the mixture to begin to boil. Make sure to stir often. Remove from the heat and allow to cool completely. Once cool, transfer the mixture to a blender along with the tequila, orange liqueur, and a single lime slice. Blend until smooth.

2. Fill a Popsicle mold with a few slices of lemon and lime slices and then pour the mixture into each mold, dividing evenly among all the molds.

3. Place the lid on top and stick in the Popsicle sticks. Freeze overnight or until completely frozen. Unmold and sprinkle with salt before serving.

english
wassail

i'm going to go ahead and say that my wassail is the stuff of legend. I got the recipe years ago from a friend and continue to make adjustments to it every winter to keep improving the recipe. By "make adjustments," I mean that I basically just keep upping the amount of brandy. Nobody is complaining. Because this drink is rich in flavor and since it's toasty warm, it's perfect for winter. For our holiday party every year, I make a big batch and then serve it chilled and topped with champagne. So many uses, all of them delicious.

Makes 6 to 8 servings

INGREDIENTS

1 gallon real apple cider (not from concentrate, not apple juice)
1 (750-ml) bottle brandy
1 tablespoon whole cloves
1 tablespoon whole allspice berries
4 cinnamon sticks
5 dashes of bitters
3 oranges
Orange peel, for garnish
Fresh cranberries, for garnish

PREPARATION

1. In a large stockpot, combine the cider, brandy, cloves, allspice, cinnamon, and bitters. Stir together and heat to a slow boil over medium-high heat.

2. Cut the oranges in half and place them into the pot. Lower the heat to a simmer and allow all the ingredients to mix and mingle for at least 4 hours (this is a great recipe for a crockpot).

3. Strain all of the solid items and serve the warm yummy wassail with an orange peel garnish and some fresh cranberries.

we named this guy jorge, and he's become a mascot at chic hq

I found this vintage green dress at the goodwill as a teenager and wore it to prom - it's still one of my party go-to's

parties

Having planned 9,000 parties in my life it shouldn't come as a surprise that parties are one of my favorite things on the planet. In fact, I think food and parties are totally best friends, and best friends stick together. In this chapter I tried really hard to pick parties that you *already throw*, such as a book club or a baby shower. I will never understand an entertaining book that shows you how to throw something grandiose like a Moroccan-themed dinner party . . . because seriously, outside of Morocco, where is that actually happening? And even more so, who has the time? What you'll find on these pages are some of my favorite party themes. I hope they encourage you and inspire some ideas for your next shindig. Just remember, you don't have to do everything all at once. Try adding a single fun new element to your next event, and I promise you'll see how much even the smallest thing can enhance the overall feel.

PARTIES

BABY *shower*

be it a bridal shower or baby shower,
there's a good chance you're going to host one, attend one, or be thrown one at some point in your lifetime. I think the key to a gorgeous party is one that focuses on the person you're celebrating rather than *what* you're celebrating. If the mother-to-be loves the color pink and is a French major who met her husband in Paris, you already have a much cooler inspiration for a theme than covering everything in baby food jars. By seeking out who someone is, you truly celebrate them in a unique and special way.

//

1. A box, basket, or bowl filled with seasonal fruit and some seasonal blooms can be the most gorgeous centerpiece and looks so feminine.

2. Serve the salad in dainty little teacups because, well, it's darling.

3. Freeze edible flowers or fruit into your ice cubes for an added pop of chic.

4. Make some jam (or buy some) using the same seasonal fruit you have in your centerpiece. It makes the perfect party favor for guests.

5

6

5. Serve your punch with edible flowers for a bit of whimsy.

6. Ask guests to fill out an "encouragement card" for the new mama. It's something she can read when she's having a sleepless night with her newborn.

7. I love the idea of having floral crowns or combs or even wrist corsages for everyone to wear to match the guest of honor's floral crown. It makes the whole party prettier and more festive.

7

park *party*

growing up we only ever had two kinds of birthday parties: an at-home party or an at-the-park party. Park birthday parties are awesome because there's so much space for kids to run around and, well, the park is free. Since it's still a popular location for many families to celebrate, here are some ideas to help you personalize the space.

1. Use the park table if possible and cover it to make it a little chicer. I use a drop cloth from the hardware store. It costs five dollars and has the perfect taupe color.

2. Use a cookie cutter to create the birthday year for your fruit salad—so cute!

3. Don't forget a hand-washing station for your littles!

4. A cupcake wrapper garland is easy to make, lightweight, and adds darling personality to your table or can be easily hung in the trees.

5. Prepack your utensils and napkins in brown paper bags or cute envelopes.

6. Put your salad in big glass jars for cute service—these are actually drink dispensers!

1

patriotic
party

i mentioned before how much

I've always loved the Fourth of July. It's such a fun addition to summer and I can't help feeling so proud to be an American each time it comes around. Since these party ideas are based on a red, white, and blue color scheme you can also use them for Memorial Day or Labor Day, or to celebrate your favorite member of the military.

1. Any cake gets into the spirit with some simple sticker cake toppers.

2. Set your buffet up the easy way. Put each guests' silverware and napkin inside their drinking glass and place them at the end of the table for easy access.

3. Add some bows to the end of your sparklers to make them look cuter in the display.

4. Prepack your Patriotic Punch (pg. 201) and keep it on ice so guests can grab and go.

5. Best dishes to serve for the 4th? Jell-O Pretzel Salad (pg. 171) and Chili Cheese Dip (pg. 56) of course!

sunday supper

2

dinner on sundays is kind of sacred. It's a special time to get together and enjoy a meal before you head off into the chaos of a hectic week. I love to use it as an open invitation to any of our friends and family to stop by and enjoy dinner with us. My favorite food to serve is fried chicken and mac 'n' cheese, but we've also had Sunday suppers where we ordered pizza to make it easier on ourselves. The goal is to connect with your loved ones over food—what you eat is almost irrelevant.

1. For a fun switcheroo, set a low table with pillows all around. A piece of plywood and some cinder blocks look totally chic when you put a linen tablecloth on top.

2. Get creative with your place card. I've written guests' names on everything from rocks, to fruit, to tea bags. It's a simple thing, but it adds a sweet surprise to the table.

3. Pull pillows from your house to create this look. Don't want them to get dirty? Put down a blanket or rug first and set up the table on top.

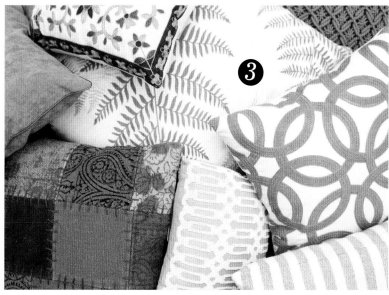

3

4. Don't forget a favor . . . little jars of homemade moonshine (pg. 205) are just the ticket.

5. You don't need anything to match. In fact, I think this party is so much more charming because it feels comfortable and unfussy.

Menu

baked blueberry brie
pg. 52

balsamic pot roast
pg. 113

no-bake cheesecakes
pg. 181

summer
cocktails

❶

❷

when most people think cocktail party they think dark and brooding, but I love the colors of summer. Deep grassy greens, lemony yellows, or playful pinks: colors so bright and happy you can almost smell them through the picture. Start with a crisp base color like white linens or even bare wood and pair it with vibrant summer hues. Think votive candles and tons of glassware, floating orchids and succulents scattered throughout, your gorgeous self in a fabulous empire waist cocktail dress with a tart martini in hand . . . it just sounds fabulous.

I popped our lemon-lime margarita popsicles (page 209) into these summer cocktails. when they melt you'll get an extra shot of tequllia! xo

///

1. Create a make-your-own cocktail bar. It gives guests something fun and interactive to do and makes for a pretty display.

❸

2. A submerged centerpiece is the easiest decoration ever. Use three different glass vases of varying heights filled with water and flowers. Anyone can do it.

3. Votive candles are my greatest little trick. I put them here and there for every party tucked alongside some seasonal blooms.

shopping PARTY

jewelry, clothes, makeup,

kitchen gadgets, and even essential oils . . . it seems everyone is hosting parties right now where their girlfriends come over to their house to shop. Most people might just put out an appetizer platter and call it good, but there are some great ways to personalize the event and make it easier to set up. I thought I'd show off a jewelry party (because I love baubles so much), but these ideas can easily be translated to any product.

1. Set up a table that makes it easy to shop and sip at the same time.

2. Use costume jewelry to adorn your table signage—très chic!

3. Mimosa bars are fun. Fill glass containers with a few different juices to mix with champagne or sparkling water and serve fruit to garnish.

4. Don't forget a mirror so guests can try on the items . . . and don't forget to make it look just as cute as everything else.

5. Be mindful of what you serve. Nobody wants greasy fingers if they're picking up jewelry, and nobody wants sauces and spreads served if there are clothes around that can easily be stained.

6. Need some menu inspiration? Consider light options like Fruit Salad with Raspberry Dressing (pg. 137), Chinese Chicken Salad (pg. 122) and Orange Sherbet Church Punch (pg. 199).

POT*luck*

Warm
Side Dishes

when you're hosting a potluck you can choose a theme (*Everyone bring Mexican food!*), or even tell people exactly what you need (*Who wants to sign up to make the fruit salad?*). But I personally love an old-school potluck where there's no rhyme or reason to what's on the table and your meal is a menagerie of side salads, deviled eggs, and too many starch-based recipes to count. Regardless of the theme, the key to hosting a potluck well is planning ahead. Know who is bringing what and where your extra serving spoons are. Do you have a power strip handy if more than one guest brings a slow cooker? Who's on cleanup duty? Do you have to-go containers to distribute the leftovers? A few simple tricks will make for an easy and fun potluck.

1. I put my buffet plates and silverware in a tray, box, or basket. It looks so much neater on the table.

2. Set out a stack of plates and platters for guests to use if they need to—extra credit if they all match.

3. I like to make one large centerpiece to anchor the table. My go-to? Branches from my backyard or a big bunch of herbs.

4. Create cute little signage so guests know what dishes to place where.

5. Don't forget some to-go boxes so guests can enjoy the leftovers.

Warm Side Dishes

book
CLUB

if you regularly read the chic site

or follow me on social media then you know that my love for books is topped only by my love for my family (and it's a close call). I love to read more than just about anything, so a book club gathering is almost as special as a birthday party. Plus, since most book club members take turns hosting, chances are you'll only do it once or twice a year. So why not make it into something extra special for you and your friends?

//

1. Easiest party decor ever? Grab stacks of books and put your appetizers on top! I like to use vintage books or contemporary books that all have the same color scheme.

2. Put your centerpieces in old tea tins or even empty soup cans; it adds a fun vintage feel. Don't have a centerpiece? Use some clippings from your yard.

3. I buy linen cocktail napkins when I find them on clearance and use them for occasions like this. Who cares if I don't have the whole alphabet?

4. Every great party needs a signature drink. Name yours after your favorite literary character.

don't the blt bites look so cute up there? find them on page 42. xo

*tail*gate

i'll be honest—at a tailgate party, I just show up for the food. I wish I loved any sport enough to want to gather in the fall in a parking lot and hang out before the game starts. I don't. But I do love tailgate food and tailgate accessories and all the fun you can have prepping the food and choosing the menu. Plus, big-time tailgaters do it every weekend, so that means an entire season of perfecting each element of your setup. Originally I wanted us to shoot this party using a cool vintage truck . . . because I'm a dreamer like that. But then I realized very few people get to tailgate in an old vintage truck, so let's keep it real. This is literally set up in the back of my real-life mom car. And if I can make that look cute, so can you.

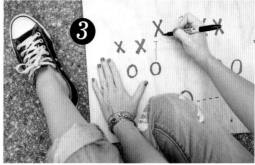

1. Chips or popcorn can be served in our DIY football bags. Just fill them up last thing because grease can stain the bag (which isn't cute).

2. Use custom stickers and your mad computer skills to create designs for your cups. This could be your team's logo or your own monogram.

3. Use a Sharpie on a big piece of plywood to write out football plays. This serves as a solid surface for all of your treats and can be used over and over. PS—I have no idea if these are real plays; I'm only here for the food, remember?

4. Attach your bottle opener to the side of your drink tub with a cute ribbon so you won't lose it.

5. Prepackage your main dish so guests can grab easily. Get my Turkey Chili recipe on page 105.

6. Put your small toppings in an old muffin tray . . . because it's adorable.

7. We have hot chocolate in our cups, but warm English Wassail (pg. 211) would be just as delicious.

8. My favorite tailgate nibbles? Pot Roast Hand Pies (pg. 154) and Missouri Cookies (pg.175).

holiday
PARTY

1

our annual holiday party is a long-standing tradition and an absolute blast. Each year we pick a fun theme (one year was Hipster Coffee Shop, another time we turned our house into a ski lodge) and invite basically everyone we've ever known over for the fun. Regardless of how you decorate, though, some essentials are always in play at a great holiday party: good food, a signature cocktail, an activity, and an opportunity to give back. This is how we celebrate the season.

1. Make sure you plan out your timeline and include time for yourself to get dressed. There's nothing worse than a gorgeous party where you're just stepping into the shower five minutes before it starts.

2. Again, the votives and seasonal blooms make an appearance. I'm telling you, this is standard!

3. I call these Wassail Sippers . . . it's my wassail topped off with champagne and garnished with some cranberries. So fantastic!

4. Every holiday party we throw is also a food drive for our local food pantry. In the party invitation, we ask guests to bring nonperishables, and we are always so amazed at everyone's generosity.

5. Consider appetizers that you can serve at room temperature so you don't have to babysit your menu all night.

acknowledgments

Guys, I wrote a cookbook! Can you even believe it? I'm still in total shock about all of this, so bear with me while I freak out over all the people who helped me make this thing real.

I know people always say, *This book wouldn't be possible without blah, blah, blah,* but seriously, this book would not be possible if it weren't for the incredible talent of Cortnee Brown and Jonathan Melendez.

Jonathan, you are the most incredible food stylist and photographer the world has ever known! Thank you for always taking my harebrained recipe ideas and helping me turn them into something beautiful.

Cortnee, if it weren't for your attention to detail and incredible design aesthetic I'd still be a baby blogger who thinks Comic Sans is a classy font. Thank you for taking my vision and turning it into reality. I'm never totally sure how to say what I want it to look like and yet you understand me just the same.

Thank you to my editor, Kat Brzozowski, for taking a chance on this idea…and for pointing out that imitation cherry doesn't actually taste like real cherries at all.

Thank you to Kevan Lyon and Kathleen Rushall, for helping me get from concept to publication. This book is literally a lifelong dream come true and I couldn't have asked for better champions.

Shout out to Erica Espana from Twine Events, former assistant/current hugely talented event planner, who helped give life and dimension to all the parties in here.

Big thanks to my friends at Ixora Florist, for all the gorgeous centerpieces…they smelled as pretty as they looked.

Michelle Lopez, you are an entire support staff all wrapped up in one amazing woman. I could not run my life or my business without your invaluable help. Thank you for all you do.

Thank you to each member of my family who loaned out their recipes in this book: Aunt Linda, Mom, Daddy, Uncle Joe, Grandma Neeley, Mema, my mother-in-law Patty, and my big sisters Melody and Christina.

And lastly—because you save the last thank-you for the most important people—all my love to Jackson, Sawyer, Ford, and Dave Hollis. There is no greater joy in my life than to be gathered around our table. Thank you for being my first, and most important, test kitchen.

XO, Rach

index

Q

R